D0463489

The Glenstal Book of Prayer

'Jesus Christ Blessing'
In the Icon Chapel at Glenstal Abbey.

Come to me, all you that are weary
and are carrying heavy burdens,
and I will give you rest.
Mt 11:28

'First of all, with instant prayer, beg that He would bring to completion every good you set out to do.'

Prologue to the Rule of St Benedict

The Glenstal
Book of Prayer

A BENEDICTINE PRAYER BOOK

THE LITURGICAL PRESS
Collegeville, Minnesota
www.litpress.org

Published in the United States of America and in Canada by
THE LITURGICAL PRESS
Collegeville, Minnesota 56321

Designed by Bill Bolger
The cover icon is of St Nicholas, from the early nineteenth
century, Jaroslavl School, in the Icon Chapel at Glenstal Abbey
Origination by The Columba Press
Printed in the United States of America

ISBN 0-8146-2767-6

Acknowledgements

Grateful acknowledgement is made to the following for permission to use copyright material: Biblibal quotations are from the *New Revised Standard Version,* copyright © 1989, by the Division of Christian Education of the National Council of the Churches of Christ in the USA, and are used by permission; Excerpts from the English translation of *The Roman Missal* © 1973, International Committe on English in the Liturgy, Inc. All rights reserved; English translation of the *Benedictus* and the *Magnificat* by the International Consultation on English Texts; The translations of the Psalms are used by permission of The Grail (England) and in the USA of GIA Publications Inc, Chicago, Ill.; Foilseacháin Ábhar Spioradálta for prayers from *Ár bPaidreacha Dúchais* by Diarmuid Ó Laoghaire; Veritas Publications for a translation from *Prayers of Two Peoples* by Fr Stephen Redmond SJ; Dominican Publications for prayers from *Proclaiming All Your Wonders*; Four Courts Press for quotations from *The Rule of St Benedict,* trs The Monks of Glenstal (1994). The Stations of the Cross are adapted from the texts by Pope John Paul II for the millennium, published in *Osservatore Romano.*

Copyright © 2001, Glenstal Abbey

Contents

Section 3: Ritual Prayers

Prayers for Various Occasions

Introduction

'Prayer is the highest achievement of which the human person is capable.' (St Teresa Benedicta of the Cross, Edith Stein)

Prayer is the movement of the Holy Spirit in the human heart through which God reaches out and embraces human beings. It is a duet of love in which the action of the Spirit inspires and sustains us in the darkness of faith. It is an inward call from Christ who dwells within the depths of the human soul, and who longs to be known and loved there. It is the exciting adventure of the search for God's presence and the endless joy of rejoicing in it when it is found. It is the growing perception of the infinitely gracious, infinitely merciful Source, the Father who reveals the beauty of his face to the inner eye of the heart and the sweetness of his voice to the inner ear attuned to listen.

The Glenstal Book of Prayer is a rich resource for the dark, mysterious, but exciting journey which is prayer. It draws on things both old and new: on the wisdom of the Bible, enshrined in Benedictine liturgy, on the experience of modern monks, and on the wisdom of the Christian church throughout her long and varied history. Coming as it does from an Irish monastery it reflects in a special way the Celtic tradition with its earthy, popular and devotional prayers.

The first section of the book is a simple 'Liturgy of the Hours'. This is used to dedicate and bless those two great moments of the day that bear witness to Christ: morning, when we celebrate his rising as the light of the world, and evening, when we acclaim him as the unquenchable light which never sets. Through psalms, canticles and other words of scripture, through invocations and concluding prayers, the day is hallowed and the presence of the risen Christ is gratefully remembered.

In addition, elements have been included stemming from the ancient custom of consecrating special moments to the Lord in the bustle of the daily round. 'Prayer-stops' are the modern equivalent of monastic 'Little Hours,' recalling as they do the coming of the Holy Spirit and the dramatic events of Christ's passion. They are an invitation and an opportunity to pause in the midst of work and turn our hearts to God. Night prayer (Compline), the last monastic office of the day, is included as the prayer before sleep. Its haunting psalms and canticles, its prayers for protection, its calling upon Mary, are some of the most beautiful treasures from the storehouse of monastic prayer. They lead us gently across the bridge of sleep, from the glaring light of day to the dark cradle of the night and the world of dreams.

This liturgical section includes a seasonal element so that the great festivals of the Christian year may be incorporated in our prayer. A selection of prayers for that purpose is also provided. These can be used in place of the prayer at the end of morning and evening prayer.

The second section consists of familiar prayers, those tried and tested prayer texts stretching back through the centuries: the Lord's Prayer, the Apostles' Creed, the Stations of the Cross, the Rosary and many others.

The third section, ritual prayers, provides formulae for various needs and occasions as they arise in every life, and a series of blessings. It will be a valuable and useful resource for the many times when spoken or formal prayers are looked for in situations of necessity, sorrow, joy or grief. The Celtic element is particularly marked in this part of the book. There is also a special prayer for Benedictine Oblates.

The fourth part includes psalms (to supplement the liturgical section or for meditation) and a series of quotations from the Rule of Saint Benedict. The latter, encapsulating the wisdom of this great foundational text of Christian civilisation, can be read as part of night prayer (Compline) or simply meditated or ruminated on as a source of inspiration in one's spiritual life. The fifth and final section includes a calendar of saints and feast days.

Thus the whole sweep of prayer from the needs of the individual to the rhythms of the day and night are provided for. Our hope is that the duet sung by the Spirit and the human heart can expand into a cosmic hymn of praise to God, Creator, Redeemer and Sanctifier of the world. Then the goal of Benedict himself will be fulfilled and God will be glorified in all things. 'Let us lift up our hearts and give thanks to the Lord our God!'

SECTION ONE   DAILY PRAYER

Daily Prayer: Sunday Morning

In the name of the Father, and of the Son, and of the
Holy Spirit. Amen.

Morning invocation of the light

> Glory be to God who has shown us the light!
> Lead me from darkness to light,
> Lead me from sadness to joy,
> Lead me from death to immortality.
> Glory be to God who has shown us the light!

Psalm 62

> *To you, O God, I keep vigil at dawn, to look upon your*
> *power, alleluia.*

O God, you are my God, for you I long;
> for you my soul is thirsting.
My body pines for you
like a dry, weary land without water.
So I gaze on you in the sanctuary
to see your strength and your glory.

For your love is better than life,
my lips will speak your praise.
So I will bless you all my life,
in your name I will lift up my hands.

My soul shall be filled as with a banquet,
my mouth shall praise you with joy.
On my bed I remember you.
On you I muse through the night
for you have been my help;
in the shadow of your wings I rejoice.
My soul clings to you;
your right hand holds me fast.

Glory be.

Scripture Reading
Rev 7:10-12
'Salvation belongs to our God who sits upon the throne,
and to the Lamb!' And all the angels stood round the
throne and round the elders and the four living creatures,
and they fell on their faces before the throne and wor-
shiped God, saying, 'Amen! Blessing and glory and wisdom and thanksgiving and honor and power and might
be to our God for ever and ever! Amen.'

Pause for silent prayer

Canticle of Zechariah (Benedictus)

'May that morning star which never sets, Christ our light,
find us aflame with charity until the world is enlightened
with love.' (St Bede)

Lk 1:68-79

Blessed be the Lord, the God of Israel;
he has come to his people and set them free.
He has raised up for us a mighty saviour,
born of the house of his servant David.

Through his holy prophets he promised of old
    that he would save us from our enemies,
from the hands of all who hate us.
He promised to show mercy to our fathers
and to remember his holy covenant.

This was the oath he swore to our father Abraham:
to set us free from the hands of our enemies,
free to worship him without fear,
holy and righteous in his sight all the days of our life.

You, my child, shall be called the prophet of the Most High
for you will go before the Lord to prepare his way,
to give his people knowledge of salvation
by forgiving them their sins.

In the tender compassion of our God
the dawn from on high shall break upon us,
to shine on those who dwell in darkness
    and the shadow of death,
and to guide our feet on the road of peace.

Glory be.

Invocations

> We welcome you, Lord, with joy and praise:
>> Let us rise with you to the light of Easter.
> Help us to see your goodness in all creatures:
>> Open our hearts to your love in the world.
> We pray for all Christian communities:
>> Deepen their faith in unity and love.

The Lord's Prayer

Concluding prayer

> Father of mercy,
> your love embraces everyone
> and through the resurrection of your Son
> you call us all into your wonderful light.
> Dispel our darkness
> and make us a people with one heart and one voice,
> forever singing your praise,
> in Jesus, the Christ, our Lord. Amen.

Blessing

> May Christ our Lord, by the power of his resurrection
> have mercy on us and save us. Amen.

> May the souls of the faithful departed through the
> mercy of God rest in peace. Amen.

> Saint (of the day) Guí orainn / Pray for us.

Daily Prayer: Sunday Evening

In the name of the Father, and of the Son, and of the
Holy Spirit. Amen.

Evening praise for the light

    O joyful light of the holy glory of the immortal Father,
    heavenly, holy, blessed Jesus Christ!
    Now that we have come to the sun's hour of rest,
    the lights of evening round us shine.
    We praise the Father, the Son and the Holy Spirit,
    One God.
    Worthy are you, O Lord,
    at all times to be praised with undefiled tongue,
    O Son of God, O giver of life!
    Therefore you are glorified throughout the universe.

Psalm 85

    *Blessed are those who hunger and thirst for righteousness, for
    they will be filled. (Mt 5:6)*

    Turn your ear, O Lord, and give answer
       for I am poor and needy.
    Preserve my life for I am faithful;
    save the servant who trusts in you.

    You are my God, have mercy on me, Lord,
    for I cry to you all the day long.
    Give joy to your servant, O Lord,
    for to you I lift up my soul.

O Lord, you are good and forgiving,
Full of love to all who call.
Give heed, O Lord, to my prayer
and attend to the sound of my voice.

I will praise you, Lord my God, with all my heart
and glorify your name for ever;
for your love to me has been great;
you have saved me from the depths of the grave.

Glory be.

Scripture Reading
2 Cor 1:3-4
Blessed be the God and Father of our Lord Jesus Christ,
the Father of mercies and the God of all consolation, who
consoles us in all our affliction, so that we may be able to
console those in any affliction with the consolation with
which we ourselves are consoled by God.

Pause for silent prayer

Canticle of Mary (Magnificat)

> *'Let the soul of Mary be in each one of you to magnify the
> Lord. Let the spirit of Mary be in each one to exult in God.'*
> *(St Ambrose)*

Lk 1:46-55

My soul proclaims the greatness of the Lord,
my spirit rejoices in God my Saviour;
for he has looked with favour on his lowly servant,
and from this day all generations will call me blessed.

The Almighty has done great things for me:
holy is his Name.
He has mercy on those who fear him
in every generation.

He has shown the strength of his arm,
he has scattered the proud in their conceit.
He has cast down the mighty from their thrones,
and has lifted up the lowly.
He has filled the hungry with good things,
and has sent the rich away empty.

He has come to the help of his servant Israel
for he has remembered his promise of mercy,
the promise he made to our fathers,
to Abraham and his children for ever.

Glory be.

Intercessions

> Christ who suffered and died for your church,
> Show us the light of your resurrection,
> Bring to the sick your comfort and healing,
> Strengthen them through the victory of the cross.
> Be near us this evening, Christ our Lord,
> Save us from all dangers that threaten us.

The Lord's Prayer

Concluding prayer

> We give you thanks, Lord our God,
> for this day, now drawing to a close.
> May our prayer, rising before you like incense,
> be pleasing to you;
> and may our outstretched hands
> be filled with your mercy,
> through Jesus, your Son, our Lord. Amen.

Blessing

May Christ our Lord, by the power of his resurrection have mercy on us and save us. Amen.

May the souls of the faithful departed through the mercy of God rest in peace. Amen.

Saint (of the day) Guí orainn/Pray for us.

Daily Prayer: Monday Morning

In the name of the Father, and of the Son, and of the
Holy Spirit. Amen.

Morning invocation of the light
> Glory be to God who has shown us the light!
> Lead me from darkness to light,
> Lead me from sadness to joy,
> Lead me from death to immortality.
> Glory be to God who has shown us the light!

Psalm 5:2-10, 12-13
> *Those who have received the word of God which dwells
> within will live for ever.*

To my words give ear, O Lord,
give heed to my groaning.
Attend to the sound of my cries,
my King and my God.

It is you whom I invoke, O Lord,
in the morning you hear me;
in the morning I offer you my prayer,
watching and waiting.

You are no God who loves evil;
no sinner is your guest.
The boastful shall not stand their ground
before your face.

You hate all who do evil:
you destroy all who lie.
Deceitful and bloodthirsty people
are hateful to you, Lord.

But I through the greatness of your love
have access to your house.
I bow down before your temple,
filled with awe.
Lead me, Lord, in your justice
because of those who lie in wait;
make clear your way before me.

No truth can be found in their mouths,
their heart is all mischief,
their throat a wide-open grave,
all honey their speech.

All those you protect shall be glad
and ring out their joy.
You shelter them; in you they rejoice,
those who love your name.

Lord, it is you who bless the upright;
you surround them with favour as with a shield.

Glory be.

Scripture Reading

Rom 13:12

The night is far gone, the day is near. Let us then lay aside
the works of darkness and put on the armour of light.

Pause for silent prayer

Canticle of Zechariah (Benedictus)

> *'Christ is the Morning Star who, when the night of this world is past, brings to his saints, the promise of the light of life and opens everlasting day.' (St Bede on the Apocalypse)*
> Lk 1:68-79

Blessed be the Lord, the God of Israel;
he has come to his people and set them free.
He has raised up for us a mighty saviour,
born of the house of his servant David.

Through his holy prophets he promised of old
that he would save us from our enemies,
from the hands of all who hate us.
He promised to show mercy to our fathers
and to remember his holy covenant.

This was the oath he swore to our father Abraham:
to set us free from the hands of our enemies,
free to worship him without fear,
holy and righteous in his sight all the days of our life.

You, my child, shall be called the prophet of the Most High
for you will go before the Lord to prepare his way,
to give his people knowledge of salvation
by forgiving them their sins.

In the tender compassion of our God
the dawn from on high shall break upon us,
to shine on those who dwell in darkness
and the shadow of death,
and to guide our feet on the road of peace.

Glory be.

Intercessions

> Christ the eternal priest:
>> Offer our lives to the Father.
> Lord you are love itself:
>> Grant that we may love you.
> Give us today the fruits of the Holy Spirit:
>> Make us gentle and kind.

The Lord's Prayer

Concluding prayer

> Lord Jesus, eternal splendour,
> on this day which is given us by the Father's love,
> do not let us lose sight of you
> but always bring us back to the light of your face,
> for you live and reign for ever and ever. Amen.

Blessing

May God the Father and the Son bless us in the unity of the Holy Spirit. Amen.

May the souls of the faithful departed through the mercy of God rest in peace. Amen.

Saint (of the day) Guí orainn / Pray for us.

Daily Prayer: Monday Evening

In the name of the Father, and of the Son, and of the Holy Spirit. Amen.

Evening praise for the light

> O joyful light of the holy glory of the immortal Father,
> heavenly, holy, blessed Jesus Christ!
> Now that we have come to the sun's hour of rest,
> the lights of evening round us shine.
> We praise the Father, the Son and the Holy Spirit,
> One God.
> Worthy are you, O Lord,
> at all times to be praised with undefiled tongue,
> O Son of God, O giver of life!
> Therefore you are glorified throughout the universe.

Psalm 26 (first part)

> *And I heard a loud voice from the throne saying, 'See, the home of God is among mortals.' (Rev 21:3)*

> The Lord is my light and my help;
> whom shall I fear?
> The Lord is the stronghold of my life;
> before whom shall I shrink?

> When evil-doers draw near
> to devour my flesh,
> it is they, my enemies and foes,
> who stumble and fall.

Though an army encamp against me
my heart would not fear.
Though war break out against me
even then I would trust.

There is one thing I ask of the Lord,
for this I long,
to live in the house of the Lord,
all the days of my life,
to savour the sweetness of the Lord,
to behold his temple.

For there he keeps me safe in his tent
in the day of evil.
He hides me in the shelter of his tent,
on a rock he sets me safe.

And now my head shall be raised
above my foes who surround me,
and I shall offer within his tent a sacrifice of joy.
I will sing and make music for the Lord.

Glory be.

Scripture Reading

Rom 8:26-28

The Spirit helps us in our weakness; for we do not know
how to pray as we ought, but that very Spirit intercedes
with sighs too deep for words. And God, who searches the
heart, knows what is the mind of the Spirit, because the
Spirit intercedes for the saints according to the will of God.

Pause for silent prayer

Canticle of Mary (Magnificat)

'God's greatest gifts fall into hearts that are empty of self.'
(St John of the Cross)

Lk 1:46-55

My soul proclaims the greatness of the Lord,
my spirit rejoices in God my Saviour;
for he has looked with favour on his lowly servant,
and from this day all generations will call me blessed.

The Almighty has done great things for me:
holy is his Name.
He has mercy on those who fear him
in every generation.

He has shown the strength of his arm,
he has scattered the proud in their conceit.
He has cast down the mighty from their thrones,
and has lifted up the lowly.
He has filled the hungry with good things,
and has sent the rich away empty.

He has come to the help of his servant Israel
for he has remembered his promise of mercy,
the promise he made to our fathers,
to Abraham and his children for ever.

Glory be.

Invocations

Lord Jesus, grant that the whole world may be saved:

Bring all people to the knowledge of your truth.

Lord, in your kindness be with the poor and weak:

Bring them the help of your comfort.

Lord, bring your healing to the sick:

Give food and drink to the hungry and thirsty.

The Lord's Prayer

Concluding prayer

In the peace of evening,

we come to you, Lord God.

May your word free our hearts

from the cares of this day.

As we experience your forgiveness in Jesus,

may we too forgive in him

our brothers and sisters who have injured us.

We ask this in his name,

Jesus, the Christ, our Lord. Amen.

Blessing

May God the Father and the Son bless us in the unity of the Holy Spirit. Amen.

May the souls of the faithful departed through the mercy of God rest in peace. Amen.

Saint (of the day) Guí orainn / Pray for us.

Daily Prayer: Tuesday Morning

In the name of the Father, and of the Son, and of the
Holy Spirit. Amen.

Morning invocation of the light

> Glory be to God who has shown us the light!
> Lead me from darkness to light,
> Lead me from sadness to joy,
> Lead me from death to immortality.
> Glory be to God who has shown us the light!

Psalm 22

For the lamb at the centre of the throne will be their shep-
herd, and he will guide them to springs of the water of life.
(Rev 7:17)

The Lord is my shepherd;
there is nothing I shall want.
Fresh and green are the pastures
where he gives me repose.

Near restful waters he leads me,
to revive my drooping spirit.
He guides me along the right path;
he is true to his name.

If I should walk in the valley of darkness
no evil would I fear.
You are there with your crook and your staff;
with these you give me comfort.

You have prepared a banquet for me
in the sight of my foes.
My head you have anointed with oil;
my cup is overflowing.

Surely goodness and kindness shall follow me
all the days of my life.
In the Lord's own house shall I dwell
for ever and ever.

Glory be.

Scripture Reading
1 Thess 5:4-5
But you, beloved, are not in darkness, for that day to
surprise you like a thief; for you are all children of the
light and children of the day; we are not of the night or
of darkness.

Pause for silent prayer

Canticle of Zechariah (Benedictus)

'So we have the prophetic message more fully confirmed. You will do well to be attentive to this as to a lamp shining in a dark place, until the day dawns and the morning star rises in your hearts.' (2 Pet 1:19)

Lk 1:68-79

Blessed be the Lord, the God of Israel;
he has come to his people and set them free.
He has raised up for us a mighty saviour,
born of the house of his servant David.

Through his holy prophets he promised of old
    that he would save us from our enemies,
from the hands of all who hate us.
He promised to show mercy to our fathers
and to remember his holy covenant.

This was the oath he swore to our father Abraham:
to set us free from the hands of our enemies,
free to worship him without fear,
holy and righteous in his sight all the days of our life.

You, my child, shall be called the prophet of the Most High
for you will go before the Lord to prepare his way,
to give his people knowledge of salvation
by forgiving them their sins.

In the tender compassion of our God
the dawn from on high shall break upon us,
to shine on those who dwell in darkness
    and the shadow of death,
and to guide our feet on the road of peace.

Glory be.

Invocations
    Strengthen in us, Lord, our love for you today:
        Lord lead us to the truth.
    We offer you our needs this morning:
        Take to yourself our cares and hopes.
    Lord Jesus, we pray for all who suffer:
        Show them your compassion through us.

The Lord's Prayer

Concluding Prayer
    Father of Jesus Christ,
    open our hearts to your word
    and to the power of the Spirit.
    Give us love to discover your will
    and strength to carry it out today;
    for you are light,
    for ever and ever. Amen.

Blessing

    May Christ, the only Son of God, bless and help us.
    Amen.

    May the souls of the faithful departed through the
    mercy of God rest in peace. Amen.

    Saint (of the day) Guí orainn/Pray for us.

Daily Prayer: Tuesday Evening

In the name of the Father, and of the Son, and of the
Holy Spirit. Amen.

Evening praise for the light

O joyful light of the holy glory of the immortal Father,
heavenly, holy, blessed Jesus Christ!
Now that we have come to the sun's hour of rest,
the lights of evening round us shine.
We praise the Father, the Son and the Holy Spirit,
One God.
Worthy are you, O Lord,
at all times to be praised with undefiled tongue,
O Son of God, O giver of life!
Therefore you are glorified throughout the universe.

Psalm 26 (second part)

Blessed be the God and Father of our Lord Jesus Christ! By his
great mercy he has given us a new birth into a living hope.
(1 Pet 1:3)

O Lord, hear my voice when I call,
have mercy and answer.
Of you my heart has spoken:
'Seek his face.'

It is your face, O Lord, that I seek;
hide not your face.
Dismiss not your servant in anger;
you have been my help.

Do not abandon or forsake me,
O God my help !
Though father and mother forsake me,
the Lord will receive me.

Instruct me, Lord, in your way;
on an even path lead me.
When they lie in ambush protect me
from my enemy's greed.
False witnesses rise against me,
breathing out fury.

I am sure I shall see the Lord's goodness
in the land of the living.
Hope in him, hold firm and take heart.
Hope in the Lord!

Glory be.

Scripture Reading

Rom 12:9-12

Let love be genuine; hate what is evil, hold fast to what is
good; love one another with mutual affection; outdo one
another in showing honour. Do not lag in zeal, be ardent
in spirit, serve the Lord. Rejoice in hope, be patient in suf-
fering, persevere in prayer.

Pause for silent prayer

Canticle of Mary (Magnificat)

> *'Christ is the image of God; hence any good or religious deed a soul has performed, magnifies the image of God in whose likeness it was made.'* (St Ambrose)

Lk 1:46-55

My soul proclaims the greatness of the Lord,
my spirit rejoices in God my Saviour;
for he has looked with favour on his lowly servant,
and from this day all generations will call me blessed.

The Almighty has done great things for me:
holy is his Name.
He has mercy on those who fear him
in every generation.

He has shown the strength of his arm,
he has scattered the proud in their conceit.
He has cast down the mighty from their thrones,
and has lifted up the lowly.
He has filled the hungry with good things,
and has sent the rich away empty.

He has come to the help of his servant Israel
for he has remembered his promise of mercy,
the promise he made to our fathers,
to Abraham and his children for ever.

Glory be.

Intercessions

> At the end of the day we give thanks to you, O Lord:
>> Glory to you, our God.
> Teach us to seek the things that please you:
>> Help us to find you in all that we do.
> Lord, feed us with bread from heaven:
>> Guide us with the light of your word.

The Lord's Prayer

Concluding prayer

> Father,
> we thank you for showing us your mercy today;
> may that mercy extend to all those
> whom you entrust to our prayer;
> and may it bring your peace to all people,
> through Jesus Christ, our Lord. Amen.

Blessing

> May Christ, the only Son of God, bless and help us.
> Amen.

> May the souls of the faithful departed through the
> mercy of God rest in peace. Amen.

> Saint (of the day) Guí orainn / Pray for us.

Daily Prayer: Wednesday Morning

In the name of the Father, and of the Son, and of the
Holy Spirit. Amen.

Morning invocation of the light

> Glory be to God who has shown us the light!
> Lead me from darkness to light,
> Lead me from sadness to joy,
> Lead me from death to immortality.
> Glory be to God who has shown us the light!

Psalm 45

> *Come, Lord Jesus. (Rev 22:20)*

God is for us a refuge and strength,
a helper close at hand, in time of distress:
so we shall not fear though the earth should rock,
though the mountains fall into the depths of the sea,
even though its waters rage and foam,
even though the mountains be shaken by its waves.

The Lord of hosts is with us:
the God of Jacob is our stronghold.
The waters of a river give joy to God's city,
the holy place where the Most High dwells.
God is within, it cannot be shaken;
God will help it at the dawning of the day.
Nations are in tumult, kingdoms are shaken:
he lifts his voice, the earth shrinks away.

The Lord of hosts is with us,
the God of Jacob is our stronghold.
Come, consider the works of the Lord,
the redoubtable deeds he has done on the earth;
the bow he breaks, the spear he snaps.
He burns the shields with fire.

'Be still and know that I am God,
supreme among the nations, supreme on the earth!'

The Lord of hosts is with us,
the God of Jacob is our stronghold.

Glory be.

Scripture Reading

Heb 1:1-2

Long ago God spoke to our ancestors in many and various
ways by the prophets, but in these last days he has spoken
to us by a Son, whom he appointed heir of all things,
through whom he also created the worlds.

Pause for silent prayer

Canticle of Zechariah (Benedictus)
*'The light of the just is the lamp that was always burning in
the tabernacle of the Covenant, and now burns also in the
church.' (St Ambrose on Psalm 118)*

   Lk 1:68-79

Blessed be the Lord, the God of Israel;
he has come to his people and set them free.
He has raised up for us a mighty saviour,
born of the house of his servant David.

Through his holy prophets he promised of old
   that he would save us from our enemies,
from the hands of all who hate us.
He promised to show mercy to our fathers
and to remember his holy covenant.

This was the oath he swore to our father Abraham:
to set us free from the hands of our enemies,
free to worship him without fear,
holy and righteous in his sight all the days of our life.

You, my child, shall be called the prophet of the Most High
for you will go before the Lord to prepare his way,
to give his people knowledge of salvation
by forgiving them their sins.

In the tender compassion of our God
the dawn from on high shall break upon us,
to shine on those who dwell in darkness
   and the shadow of death,
and to guide our feet on the road of peace.

Glory be.

Invocations

Lord Jesus, let the love of the Spirit be in us:
We consecrate our hearts to you.
Help all Christians to answer your call:
May they be a light to the world.
Bless all religious communities:
Enrich them with your gifts.

The Lord's Prayer

Concluding prayer

Father almighty,
You revealed to us that you are light.
Help us to live our lives in your radiance
And we will be in fellowship with one another
Through Jesus, the Christ, our Lord.

Blessing

May God light the fire of his love in our hearts. Amen.

May the souls of the faithful departed through the
mercy of God rest in peace. Amen.

Saint (of the day) Guí orainn/Pray for us.

Daily Prayer: Wednesday Evening

In the name of the Father, and of the Son, and of the Holy Spirit. Amen.

Evening praise for the light

O joyful light of the holy glory of the immortal Father,
heavenly, holy, blessed Jesus Christ!
Now that we have come to the sun's hour of rest,
the lights of evening round us shine.
We praise the Father, the Son and the Holy Spirit,
One God.
Worthy are you, O Lord,
at all times to be praised with undefiled tongue,
O Son of God, O giver of life!
Therefore you are glorified throughout the universe.

Psalm 137

I can do all things through him who strengthens me. (Phil 4:13)

I thank you, Lord, with all my heart,
you have heard the words of my mouth.
In the presence of the angels I will bless you.
I will adore before your holy temple.

I thank you for your faithfulness and love
which excel all we ever knew of you.
On the day I called, you answered;
you increased the strength of my soul.

All the rulers on earth shall thank you
when they hear the words of your mouth.
They shall sing of the Lord's ways:
'How great is the glory of the Lord!'

The Lord is high yet he looks on the lowly
and the haughty he knows from afar.
Though I walk in the midst of affliction
you give me life and frustrate my foes.

You stretch out your hands and save me,
your hand will do all things for me.
Your love, O Lord, is eternal,
discard not the work of your hands.

Glory be.

Scripture Reading

1 Cor 9:2

Do you not know that in a race the runners all compete,
but only one receives the prize? Run in such a way that
you may win it.

Pause for silent prayer

Canticle of Mary (Magnificat)

> *'Mary had every right to rejoice in Jesus, for in one and the same person he would truly be her Son and Saviour.' (St Bede)*
> Lk 1:46-55

My soul proclaims the greatness of the Lord,
my spirit rejoices in God my Saviour;
for he has looked with favour on his lowly servant,
and from this day all generations will call me blessed.

The Almighty has done great things for me:
holy is his Name.
He has mercy on those who fear him
in every generation.

He has shown the strength of his arm,
he has scattered the proud in their conceit.
He has cast down the mighty from their thrones,
and has lifted up the lowly.
He has filled the hungry with good things,
and has sent the rich away empty.

He has come to the help of his servant Israel
for he has remembered his promise of mercy,
the promise he made to our fathers,
to Abraham and his children for ever.

Glory be.

Invocations

> Lord, remember all who live the Christian life:
>> Show them the light of your face.
> Uphold all who serve you in the ministry:
>> Give them the strength of your Holy Spirit.
> Fill the hearts of your people with joy and peace:
>> Answer all their needs.

The Lord's Prayer

Concluding prayer

> It is for you that we live, Lord our God,
> and to you we have consecrated this day;
> perfect and purify our offering,
> so that our prayer of thanksgiving may rise to you,
> in Jesus, your Son, our Lord. Amen.

Blessing

> May God light the fire of his love in our hearts. Amen.

> May the souls of the faithful departed through the
> mercy of God rest in peace. Amen.

> Saint (of the day) Guí orainn / Pray for us.

Daily Prayer: Thursday Morning

In the name of the Father, and of the Son, and of the Holy Spirit. Amen.

Morning invocation of the light

> Glory be to God who has shown us the light!
> Lead me from darkness to light,
> Lead me from sadness to joy,
> Lead me from death to immortality.
> Glory be to God who has shown us the light!

Psalm 8

And he has put all things under his feet and has made him the head over all things for the church. (Eph 1:22)

How great is your name,
O Lord our God,
through all the earth!

Your majesty is praised above the heavens;
on the lips of children and of babes
you have found praise to foil your enemy,
to silence the foe and the rebel.

When I see the heavens, the work of your hands,
the moon and the stars which you arranged,
what are we that you should keep us in mind,
men and women that you care for them?

Yet you have made us little less than gods;
and crowned us with glory and honour,
gave us power over the works of your hand,
put all things under our feet.

How great is your name, O Lord our God,
through all the earth!

Glory be.

Scripture Reading
Tit 2:11-12
For the grace of God has appeared, bringing salvation to
all, training us to renounce impiety and worldly passions,
and in the present age to live lives that are self-controlled,
upright and godly.

Pause for silent prayer

Canticle of Zechariah (Benedictus)

'May the light of Christ, rising in glory, dispel the darkness of our hearts and minds.' (Easter Vigil)

Lk 1:68-79

Blessed be the Lord, the God of Israel;
he has come to his people and set them free.
He has raised up for us a mighty saviour,
born of the house of his servant David.

Through his holy prophets he promised of old
    that he would save us from our enemies,
from the hands of all who hate us.
He promised to show mercy to our fathers
and to remember his holy covenant.

This was the oath he swore to our father Abraham:
to set us free from the hands of our enemies,
free to worship him without fear,
holy and righteous in his sight all the days of our life.

You, my child, shall be called the prophet of the Most High
for you will go before the Lord to prepare his way,
to give his people knowledge of salvation
by forgiving them their sins.

In the tender compassion of our God
the dawn from on high shall break upon us,
to shine on those who dwell in darkness
    and the shadow of death,
and to guide our feet on the road of peace.

Glory be.

Invocations

We thank you, Lord, for coming into this world:
Keep our eyes fixed on you today.
Direct our thoughts and our words:
Teach us to know and do your will.
Be with us, Lord, as we take up our daily tasks:
Help us to recognise you in our work.

The Lord's Prayer

Concluding prayer

God our Father,
when you gave us your Son,
your light came into the world.
May we welcome him in our lives,
and thus be a light for our brothers and sisters.
We ask you this
through Jesus, the Christ, our Lord. Amen.

Blessing

May God be merciful to us and bless us. Amen.

May the souls of the faithful departed through the mercy of God rest in peace. Amen.

Saint (of the day) Guí orainn/Pray for us.

Daily Prayer: Thursday Evening

In the name of the Father, and of the Son, and of the Holy Spirit. Amen.

Evening praise for the light

O joyful light of the holy glory of the immortal Father,
heavenly, holy, blessed Jesus Christ!
Now that we have come to the sun's hour of rest,
the lights of evening round us shine.
We praise the Father, the Son and the Holy Spirit,
One God.
Worthy are you, O Lord,
at all times to be praised with undefiled tongue,
O Son of God, O giver of life!
Therefore you are glorified throughout the universe.

Psalm 61

*May the God of hope fill you with all joy and peace in
believing, so that you may abound in hope by the power of
the Holy Spirit. (Rom 15:13)*

In God alone is my soul at rest;
my help comes from him.
He alone is my rock, my stronghold,
my fortress: I stand firm.

How long will you attack me
to break me down,
as though I were a tottering wall,
or a tumbling fence?

Their plan is only to destroy:
they take pleasure in lies.
With their mouth they utter blessing
but in their heart they curse.

In God alone be at rest, my soul;
for my hope comes from him.
He alone is my rock, my stronghold,
my fortress: I stand firm.

In God is my safety and glory,
the rock of my strength.
Take refuge in God, all you people.
Trust him at all times.
Pour out your hearts before him
for God is our refuge.

Common folk are only a breath,
the great an illusion.
Placed in the scales, they rise;
they weigh less than a breath.

Do not put your trust in oppression
nor vain hopes on plunder.
Do not set your heart on riches
even when they increase.

For God has said only one thing:
only two do I know:
that to God alone belongs power
and to you, Lord, love;
and that you repay us all
according to our deeds.

Glory be.

Scripture Reading

1 Cor 15:20-22

But in fact Christ has been raised from the dead, the first fruits of those who have died. For since death came through a human being, the resurrection of the dead has also come through a human being; for as all die in Adam, so all will be made alive in Christ.

Pause for silent prayer

Canticle of Mary (Magnificat)

'Who is like the Lord, our God, the one enthroned on high who stoops down from the heights to look down, to look down upon heaven and earth?' (Psalm 112)

Lk 1:46-55

My soul proclaims the greatness of the Lord,
my spirit rejoices in God my Saviour;
for he has looked with favour on his lowly servant,
and from this day all generations will call me blessed.

The Almighty has done great things for me:
holy is his Name.
He has mercy on those who fear him
in every generation.

He has shown the strength of his arm,
he has scattered the proud in their conceit.
He has cast down the mighty from their thrones,
and has lifted up the lowly.
He has filled the hungry with good things,
and has sent the rich away empty.

He has come to the help of his servant Israel
for he has remembered his promise of mercy,
the promise he made to our fathers,
to Abraham and his children for ever.

Glory be.

Invocations

Lord you have saved us from slavery to sin:
  Give us the freedom of your children.
Help all who seek your light to find it:
  Let them be consecrated in the truth.
We remember the widowed and the orphaned:
  Comfort them in your love.

The Lord's Prayer

Concluding prayer

Lord God, ever faithful,
see us gathered before you
as the day draws to a close;
confirm our hearts in your love,
and keep alive in us
the memory of your goodness and kindness,
which have appeared in Jesus Christ, our Lord.

Blessing

May God be merciful to us and bless us. Amen.

May the souls of the faithful departed through the
mercy of God rest in peace. Amen.

Saint (of the day) Guí orainn/Pray for us.

Daily Prayer: Friday Morning

In the name of the Father, and of the Son, and of the Holy Spirit. Amen.

Morning invocation of the light
> Glory be to God who has shown us the light!
> Lead me from darkness to light,
> Lead me from sadness to joy,
> Lead me from death to immortality.
> Glory be to God who has shown us the light!

Psalm 50
We know that a person is justified not by the works of the law but through faith in Jesus Christ. (Gal 2:16)

Have mercy on me, God, in your kindness.
In your compassion blot out my offence.
O wash me more and more from my guilt
and cleanse me from my sin.

My offences truly I know them;
my sin is always before me.
Against you, you alone, have I sinned;
what is evil in your sight I have done.

That you may be justified when you give sentence
and be without reproach when you judge.
O see, in guilt I was born,
a sinner was I conceived.

Indeed you love truth in the heart;
then in the secret of my heart teach me wisdom.
O purify me, then I shall be clean;
O wash me, I shall be whiter than snow.

Make me hear rejoicing and gladness,
that the bones you have crushed may thrill.
From my sins turn away your face
and blot out all my guilt.

A pure heart create for me, O God,
put a steadfast spirit within me.
Do not cast me away from your presence,
nor deprive me of your Holy Spirit.

Give me again the joy of your help;
with a spirit of fervour sustain me,
that I may teach transgressors your ways
and sinners may return to you.

O rescue me, God, my helper,
and my tongue shall ring out your goodness.
O Lord, open my lips
and my mouth shall declare your praise.

For in sacrifice you take no delight,
burnt offering from me you would refuse;
my sacrifice, a contrite spirit,
a humbled, contrite heart you will not spurn.

In your goodness, show favour to Zion:
rebuild the walls of Jerusalem.

Then you will be pleased with lawful sacrifice,
burnt offerings wholly consumed
then you will be offered young bulls on your altar.

Glory be.

Scripture Reading
Phil 2:8-11
Being found in human form, Jesus humbled himself and
became obedient to the point of death – even death on a
cross. Therefore God has highly exalted him and gave him
the name that is above every name, so that at the name of
Jesus every knee should bend in heaven and on earth and
every tongue confess that Jesus Christ is Lord, to the
glory of God the Father.

Pause for silent prayer

Canticle of Zechariah (Benedictus)
*'O Rising Sun, you are the splendour of eternal light and the
sun of justice. O come and enlighten those who sit in darkness
and in the shadow of death.' (O Antiphon)*
    Lk 1:68-79
Blessed be the Lord, the God of Israel;
he has come to his people and set them free.
He has raised up for us a mighty saviour,
born of the house of his servant David.

Through his holy prophets he promised of old
    that he would save us from our enemies,
from the hands of all who hate us.

He promised to show mercy to our fathers
and to remember his holy covenant.

This was the oath he swore to our father Abraham:
to set us free from the hands of our enemies,
free to worship him without fear,
holy and righteous in his sight all the days of our life.

You, my child, shall be called the prophet of the Most High
for you will go before the Lord to prepare his way,
to give his people knowledge of salvation
by forgiving them their sins.

In the tender compassion of our God
the dawn from on high shall break upon us,
to shine on those who dwell in darkness
and the shadow of death,
and to guide our feet on the road of peace.

Glory be.

Invocations

Lord, you have delivered us by your sacrifice:
Help us to live by your new and eternal covenant.
We accept this new day as your gift to us:
Let us follow you in newness of life.
Through the blood and water flowing from your side:
Pour out the light of the Spirit upon us.

The Lord's Prayer

Concluding prayer

Lord Jesus,
your food was to do the will of your Father.
Make us attentive this day to the call of the Spirit,
and give us the strength to respond to him in humility,
for you are our help
for ever and ever. Amen.

Blessing

May the King of the Angels lead us to the heavenly city
on high. Amen.

May the souls of the faithful departed through the
mercy of God rest in peace. Amen.

Saint (of the day) Guí orainn/Pray for us.

Daily Prayer: Friday Evening

In the name of the Father, and of the Son, and of the
Holy Spirit. Amen.

Evening praise for the light

O joyful light of the holy glory of the immortal Father,
heavenly, holy, blessed Jesus Christ!
Now that we have come to the sun's hour of rest,
the lights of evening round us shine.
We praise the Father, the Son and the Holy Spirit,
One God.
Worthy are you, O Lord,
at all times to be praised with undefiled tongue,
O Son of God, O giver of life!
Therefore you are glorified throughout the universe.

Psalm 114

The Spirit and the Bride say 'Come'. And let every one who hears
say 'come'. And let anyone who is thirsty come. (Rev 22:17)

I love the Lord for he has heard
the cry of my appeal;
for he has turned his ear to me
in the day when I called him

They surrounded me, the snares of death,
with the anguish of the tomb;
they caught me, sorrow and distress.
I called on the Lord's name,
O Lord my God, deliver me.

How gracious is the Lord, and just;
our God has compassion.
The Lord protects the simple hearts;
I was helpless so he saved me.
Turn back, my soul, to your rest
for the Lord has been good;
he has kept my soul from death,
my eyes from tears
and my feet from stumbling.

I will walk in the presence of the Lord
in the land of the living.

Glory be.

Scripture Reading
Col 3:17
Whatever you do, in word or deed, do everything in the
name of the Lord Jesus, giving thanks to God the Father
through him.

Pause for silent prayer

Canticle of Mary (Magnificat)

'My spirit rejoices in the eternal divinity of Jesus, my saviour, whom I have conceived in time and bear in my body.'
(St Bede on Mary)

Lk 1:46-55

My soul proclaims the greatness of the Lord,
my spirit rejoices in God my Saviour;
for he has looked with favour on his lowly servant,
and from this day all generations will call me blessed.

The Almighty has done great things for me:
holy is his Name.
He has mercy on those who fear him
in every generation.

He has shown the strength of his arm,
he has scattered the proud in their conceit.
He has cast down the mighty from their thrones,
and has lifted up the lowly.
He has filled the hungry with good things,
and has sent the rich away empty.

He has come to the help of his servant Israel
for he has remembered his promise of mercy,
the promise he made to our fathers,
to Abraham and his children for ever.

Glory be.

Invocations

> The angel consoled you in the hour of your passion:
>> Comfort all those who are dying.
>
> Lord Jesus, you underwent the agony of the cross:
>> Teach us to adore your holy passion.
>
> Christ whose side was pierced with a lance:
>> Open to us the treasures of your love.

The Lord's Prayer

Concluding prayer

> May the memory of your death on the cross,
> Lord Jesus,
> confirm our hearts in faith and hope;
> then we shall live together in your love,
> waiting for your coming,
> for you are our Saviour, for ever and ever. Amen.

Blessing

> May the King of the Angels lead us to the heavenly city
> on high. Amen.

> May the souls of the faithful departed through the
> mercy of God rest in peace. Amen.

> Saint (of the day) Guí orainn / Pray for us.

Daily Prayer: Saturday Morning

In the name of the Father, and of the Son, and of the
Holy Spirit. Amen.

Morning invocation of the light

> Glory be to God who has shown us the light!
> Lead me from darkness to light,
> Lead me from sadness to joy,
> Lead me from death to immortality.
> Glory be to God who has shown us the light!

Psalm 41

*Blessed be the God and Father of our Lord Jesus Christ, the
father of mercies and the God of all consolation, who consoles
us in all our affliction. (2 Cor 1:3)*

L ike the deer that yearns
for running streams,
so my soul is yearning
for you, my God.

My soul is thirsting for God,
the God of my life;
when can I enter and see
the face of God?

My tears have become my bread,
by night, by day,
as I hear it said all the day long:
'Where is your God?'

Why are you cast down, my soul,
why groan within me?
Hope in God; I will praise him still,
my saviour and my God.

Glory be.

Scripture Reading
1 Cor 13:4-7
Love is patient; love is kind; it is not envious or boastful
or arrogant or rude. It does not insist on its own way; it
is not irritable or resentful; it does not rejoice in wrong-
doing, but rejoices in the truth. It bears all things,
believes all things, hopes all things, endures all things.

Pause for silent prayer

Canticle of Zechariah (Benedictus)
*'Do you not know, my friend, that you owe the first fruits of
your heart and voice to God? Run therefore to meet the rising
sun so that when the day dawns it may find you ready.'
(St Ambrose on Psalm 118)*

Lk 1:68-79

Blessed be the Lord, the God of Israel;
he has come to his people and set them free.
He has raised up for us a mighty saviour,
born of the house of his servant David.

Through his holy prophets he promised of old
that he would save us from our enemies,
from the hands of all who hate us.

He promised to show mercy to our fathers
and to remember his holy covenant.

This was the oath he swore to our father Abraham:
to set us free from the hands of our enemies,
free to worship him without fear,
holy and righteous in his sight all the days of our life.

You, my child, shall be called the prophet of the Most High
for you will go before the Lord to prepare his way,
to give his people knowledge of salvation
by forgiving them their sins.

In the tender compassion of our God
the dawn from on high shall break upon us,
to shine on those who dwell in darkness
    and the shadow of death,
and to guide our feet on the road of peace.

Glory be.

Invocations
    Lord Jesus, by the prayers of your mother:
        Guide and protect your church.
    Mary received the word in faith:
        Open our hearts to your will.
    Mary stood with hope by the cross:
        By her prayer strengthen our hope.

The Lord's Prayer

Concluding prayer

God our Father,
you chose Mary from the lowly among your people,
and her one desire was to be your handmaid.
Through her intercession,
grant us poverty of spirit,
and reveal to us the mysteries of your kingdom,
through Jesus, the Christ, our Lord. Amen.

Blessing

May the most holy Mother of God intercede for us
with the Lord. Amen.

May the souls of the faithful departed through the
mercy of God rest in peace. Amen.

Saint (of the day) Guí orainn / Pray for us.

Daily Prayer: Saturday Evening

In the name of the Father, and of the Son, and of the
Holy Spirit. Amen.

Evening praise for the light

O joyful light of the holy glory of the immortal Father,
heavenly, holy, blessed Jesus Christ!
Now that we have come to the sun's hour of rest,
the lights of evening round us shine.
We praise the Father, the Son and the Holy Spirit,
One God.
Worthy are you, O Lord,
at all times to be praised with undefiled tongue,
O Son of God, O giver of life!
Therefore you are glorified throughout the universe.

Psalm 15

*One night the Lord said to Paul in a vision, 'Do not be
afraid, but speak and do not be silent; for I am with you.'
(Acts 18:9-10)*

Preserve me, God, I take refuge in you.
I say to the Lord: 'You are my God.
My happiness lies in you alone.'

You have put into my heart a marvellous love
for the faithful ones who dwell in your land.
Those who choose other gods increase their sorrows.
Never will I offer their offerings of blood,
Never will I take their name upon my lips.

O Lord, it is you who are my portion and cup;
it is you yourself who are my prize.
The lot marked out for me is my delight,
welcome indeed the heritage that falls to me!

I will bless you, Lord, you give me counsel;
and even at night direct my heart.
I keep you, Lord, ever in my sight:
since you are at my right hand, I shall stand firm.

And so my heart rejoices, my soul is glad;
even my body shall rest in safety.
For you will not leave my soul among the dead,
nor let your beloved know decay.

You will show me the path of life,
the fulness of joy in your presence,
at your right hand happiness for ever.

Glory be.

Scripture Reading

1 Pet 4:11

Whoever speaks must do so as one speaking the very
words of God; whoever serves must do so with the
strength that God supplies, so that God may be glorified
in all things through Jesus Christ. To him belong the glory
and the power for ever and ever. Amen.

Pause for silent prayer

Canticle of Mary (Magnificat)

'This is the Magnificat, Mary's prayer par excellence, the
song of messianic times in which mingles the joy of the
ancient and the new Israel.' (Pope Paul VI, Marialis cultus,
section 18)

Lk 1:46-55

My soul proclaims the greatness of the Lord,
my spirit rejoices in God my Saviour;
for he has looked with favour on his lowly servant,
and from this day all generations will call me blessed.

The Almighty has done great things for me:
holy is his Name.
He has mercy on those who fear him
in every generation.

He has shown the strength of his arm,
he has scattered the proud in their conceit.
He has cast down the mighty from their thrones,
and has lifted up the lowly.
He has filled the hungry with good things,
and has sent the rich away empty.

He has come to the help of his servant Israel
for he has remembered his promise of mercy,
the promise he made to our fathers,
to Abraham and his children for ever.

Glory be.

Invocations

> King of peace, guide the actions of those who govern us:
>> Help them to defend the poor and needy.
> Make us true heralds of the gospel:
>> Fill our hearts with the joy of your peace.
> Christ, firstborn from the dead:
>> Hear the prayers of all who call upon you.

The Lord's Prayer

Concluding prayer

> God our Father,
> when Jesus was dying for us
> Mary his mother stood by his side,
> in the darkness which covered the earth.
> In the unending dawn of the resurrection,
> may she stand as a sign of our sure hope,
> that we will one day be with you,
> that Light that will shine for ever and ever. Amen.

Blessing

> Through the prayers of your most pure mother and of all your saints, Lord Jesus Christ have mercy on us and save us. Amen.

> May the souls of the faithful departed through the mercy of God rest in peace. Amen.

> Saint (of the day) Guí orainn / Pray for us.

Prayer during the day: Mid-Morning

An appeal for the Holy Spirit of Pentecost

In the name of the Father, and of the Son, and of the Holy Spirit. Amen.

Psalm 120

I lift up my eyes to the mountains:
from where shall come my help?
My help shall come from the Lord
who made heaven and earth.

May he never allow you to stumble!
Let him sleep not, your guard.
No, he sleeps not nor slumbers,
Israel's guard.

The Lord is your guard and your shade;
at your right side he stands.
By day the sun shall not smite you
nor the moon in the night.

The Lord will guard you from evil,
he will guard your soul.
The Lord will guard your going and coming
both now and for ever.

Pause for silent prayer

V. Send forth your Spirit, O Lord!
R. And renew the face of the earth!

The Lord's Prayer

Concluding Prayer
    Let us pray:
    All-holy Father,
    at this hour when the Spirit came down on the apostles,
    we ask you to help us live throughout this day
    the love that they proclaimed,
    through Jesus Christ our Lord. Amen.

May the grace of the Holy Spirit enlighten our hearts and
our senses. Amen.

Prayer during the day: Noon

In the name of the Father, and of the Son, and of the Holy Spirit. Amen.

Psalm 121

I rejoiced when I heard them say:
'Let us go to God's house.'
And now our feet are standing
within your gates, O Jerusalem.

Jerusalem is built as a city
strongly compact.
It is there that the tribes go up,
the tribes of the Lord.

For Israel's law it is,
there to praise the Lord's name.
There were set the thrones of judgment
of the house of David.

For the peace of Jerusalem pray:
'Peace be to your homes!
May peace reign in your walls,
in your palaces, peace!'

For love of my family and friends
I say 'Peace upon you!'
For love of the house of the Lord
I will ask for your good.

Pause for silent prayer

V. I will glory in the cross of our Lord Jesus Christ!
R Through whom the world is saved and set free!

The Lord's Prayer

Concluding prayer
    Let us pray:
    Lord Jesus, Saviour of the world,
    this is the hour when you were lifted up from the earth.
    By looking on your cross
    and seeing the depth of your love for us,
    may we never again stray from you,
    who reign with the Father for ever and ever. Amen.

We adore you, O Christ, and we bless you, because by your
holy cross you have redeemed the world. Amen.

Prayer during the day: Afternoon

A remembrance of Christ's death

In the name of the Father, and of the Son, and of the Holy
Spirit. Amen.

Psalm 122

To you have I lifted up my eyes,
you who dwell in the heavens:
my eyes, like the eyes of slaves
on the hands of their lords.

Like the eyes of a servant
on the hand of her mistress,
so our eyes are on the Lord our God
till he show us his mercy.

Have mercy on us, Lord, have mercy.
We are filled with contempt.
Indeed all too full is our soul
with the scorn of the rich,
the disdain of the proud.

Pause for silent prayer

V. Dying you destroyed our death;
rising you restored our life!
R. Lord Jesus, come in glory!

The Lord's Prayer

Concluding Prayer

Let us pray:
At the ninth hour, Lord Jesus,
you gave yourself into the hands of the Father.
May we welcome his will with love,
and fulfil it to the end,
as you have taught us
for ever and ever. Amen.

We venerate your cross, O Lord, we praise and glorify your holy resurrection: because of the wood of the tree, joy has come into the whole world. Amen.

Night Prayer: Compline

In the name of the Father, and of the Son, and of the Holy Spirit. Amen.

A short reading from the Rule of St Benedict (see page 139)

Examination of Conscience
After a brief period of silence say:
I confess to almighty God,
and to you, my brothers and sisters,
that I have sinned through my own fault
in my thoughts and in my words,
in what I have done,
and in what I have failed to do;
and I ask Blessed Mary, ever virgin,
all the angels and saints,
and you, my brothers and sisters,
to pray for me to the Lord our God.

May almighty God have mercy on us,
forgive us our sins,
and bring us to everlasting life. Amen.

One of the following psalm selections (A or B) is said:
A (Psalms 4 & 133)

Psalm 4

When I call, answer me, O God of justice;
from anguish you released me, have mercy and hear me!

You rebels, how long will your hearts be closed,
will you love what is futile and seek what is false?

It is the Lord who grants favours to those whom he loves;
the Lord hears me whenever I call him.
Fear him; do not sin: ponder on your bed and be still.
Make justice your sacrifice and trust in the Lord.

'What can bring us happiness?' many say.
Lift up the light of your face on us, O Lord.

You have put into my heart a greater joy
than they have from abundance of corn and new wine.

I will lie down in peace and sleep comes at once
for you alone, Lord, make me dwell in safety.

Glory be.

Psalm 133

O come, bless the Lord,
all you who serve the Lord.
Who stand in the house of the Lord,
in the courts of the house of our God.

Lift up your hands to the holy place
and bless the Lord through the night.

May the Lord bless you from Zion,
he who made both heaven and earth.

Glory be.

or B (Psalm 90)

Psalm 90

Those who dwell in the shelter of the Most High
and abide in the shade of the Almighty,
say to the Lord: 'My refuge,
my stronghold, my God in whom I trust.'

It is he who will free you from the snare
of the fowler who seeks to destroy you;
He will conceal you with his pinions
and under his wings you will find refuge.

You will not fear the terror of the night
nor the arrow that flies by day,
nor the plague that prowls in the darkness
nor the scourge that lays waste at noon.

A thousand may fall at your side,
ten thousand fall at your right,
You it will never approach;
his faithfulness is buckler and shield.

Your eyes have only to look
to see how the wicked are repaid,
you who have said: 'Lord, my refuge!'
and have made the Most High your dwelling.

Upon you no evil shall fall,
no plague approach where you dwell.
For you has he commanded his angels,
to keep you in all your ways.

They shall bear you upon their hands
lest you strike your foot against a stone.
On the lion and the viper you will tread
and trample the young lion and the dragon.

You set your love on me, so I will save you,
protect you for you know my name.
When you call I shall answer: 'I am with you.'
I will save you in distress and give you glory.

With length of days I will content you;
I shall let you see my saving power.

Glory be.

Scripture Reading
Jer 14:9
Yet you, O Lord, are in the midst of us, and we are called
by your name; do not forsake us, O Lord our God!

Responsory
R. Into your hands, O Lord, I commend my spirit.
V. You have redeemed us, O Lord God of truth. (Response)
V. Glory be to the Father and to the Son,
and to the Holy Spirit. (Response)

Canticle of Simeon (Nunc Dimittis)
Save us Lord, while we are awake; protect us while we sleep. That
we may keep watch with Christ, and rest with him in peace.
Lk 2:29-32

At last, all powerful Master,
you give leave to your servant
to go in peace, according to your promise.

For my eyes have seen your salvation
which you have prepared for all nations,
the light to enlighten the Gentiles
and give glory to Israel, your people.

Glory be.

Concluding prayer
Let us pray:
God our Father,
you have been our guide and our help
throughout this day:
stay with us now throughout the night.
May your light enlighten and purify our hearts,
and keep them vigilant in faith,
through Jesus, the Christ, our Lord. Amen.

May the Lord grant us a quiet night and a perfect end.
Amen.

A hymn in honour of Our Lady is now said:
Salve Regina/Hail, Holy Queen

Salve Regina Mater misericordiae,
Vita, dulcedo, et spes nostra, salve.

Ad te clamamus, exsules filii Hevae;

Ad te suspiramus gementes et flentes in hac lacrymarum valle. Eia ergo advocata nostra,

illos tuos misericordes oculos ad nos converte.

Et Jesum, benedictum fructum ventris tui,

nobis post hoc exilium ostende.

O Clemens, O pia,

O dulcis Virgo Maria.

Hail, Holy Queen, Mother of Mercy!

Hail, our life, our sweetness, and our hope!

To thee do we cry, poor banished children of Eve;

to thee do we send up our sighs,

mourning and weeping in this valley of tears.

Turn, then, most gracious advocate,

thine eyes of mercy toward us;

and after this our exile

show unto us the blessed fruit of thy womb, Jesus;

O clement, O loving, O sweet Virgin Mary.

Sub tuum praesidium

Sub tuum praesidium confugimus
Sancta Dei Genetrix

Nostras deprecationes, ne despicias in necessitatibus nostris.

Sed a periculis cunctis libera nos semper.

Virgo gloriosa et benedicta.

In your loving care we take refuge, O holy Mother of God.

Do not disregard our prayers in the time of our need;

But in every danger set us free,

O glorious and blessed Virgin.

Antiphon to Mary

O frondens virga, in tua nobilitate stans sicut aurora procedit. Nunc gaude et laetare et nos debiles dignare a mala consuetudine liberare atque manum tuam porrige ad erigendum nos.

O flowering, noble stem, your flower comes forth like the dawn.
Rejoice now and be glad, and free us from evil ways, weak as we are –
Stretch out your hand to lift us up.

Hildegard Von Bingen

Daily Prayer: Seasonal Prayer Cycle

In this section, a brief explanation of each season is followed by an appropriate prayer. This prayer may be used at morning and evening prayer.

Advent

The church's liturgical year begins with the season of Advent, which means arrival or coming. We recall the first coming of Christ (in the incarnation at Christmas) and anticipate his final coming (at the end of time). We celebrate with joy his daily coming in the time of the church, in word and sacrament. It is a season of hope and anticipation: purple vestments symbolise the yearning of the church and of all creation for the transforming light of Christ.

Before 17 December the emphasis falls on the second coming:
Prayer

> Ever faithful God,
> your prophets foretold the coming of the light.
> In your name they promised
> that the eyes of the blind would be opened.
> We confidently await the coming of your Son,
> and the day when he will gather all people
> to live in your light, for ever and ever. Amen

Between 17 and 25 December, we prepare for the feast of Christmas itself:

Prayer

God, Lord of eternity,
your Son came to visit us in time.
Grant to each of us the heart of a child
which never ceases to marvel at your wonders,
so that once again this day
you may find us watching in hope.
We ask you this, because of your love for us,
God blessed for ever and ever. Amen.

Christmas

At Christmas we celebrate the mystery of Jesus Christ, the Word made flesh for our salvation. In the incarnate Lord, a child held in the arms of Mary, we see our God made visible and so are caught up in love for the invisible God. The joy of Christmas overflows into the feasts of the Epiphany and the Baptism of Christ: these proclaim that the message of salvation, radiating from the chosen people, has shone upon the whole human race. This Christmas joy is reflected in the white vestments and Christmas crib.

Prayer

Lord our God,
you sent your Son, the Light of the World,
into the darkness
which covered the earth and its peoples.
May the brightness of his rising
shine in the church,
so that the nations may walk towards the light,
Jesus, the Christ, our Lord. Amen.

Lent

Lent is the forty days of preparation for the celebration of Christ's saving death and resurrection at Easter. It is a time of purification in which Christians struggle to fulfill their baptismal promises, by dying to selfishness and living for Christ. It begins with Ash Wednesday, a reminder of our mortality, but ends in the celebration of undying life at Easter. St Benedict tells his monks that life should always have a Lenten character about it, because the Christian is always journeying from the old realm of sin and death to the light and love of God's kingdom.

Prayer

God our Father,
your will is that everyone be saved and no one be lost.
You draw us to yourself by prayer and penance.
Grant that we may so follow Christ in love
that our lives may help others and our weakness never hinder them.
We make this prayer in his name,
Jesus, the Christ, our Lord. Amen.

Easter

In Holy Week, beginning with the commemoration of Christ's entry into Jerusalem on Palm Sunday, the church follows the path of Jesus from Gethsemane to Golgotha and to the glory of the resurrection. In the great three days (Holy Thursday, Good Friday and Holy Saturday) the events by which God saved us are celebrated: the gift of the holy Eucharist, the agony in the garden, the passion of the Lord, his descent into hell, and finally his rising from the dead. The joy of his Easter triumph overflows into fifty days of celebration. White vestments are worn, and alleluia is sung repeatedly. It culminates in his return to the Father at the ascension and his sending of the Holy Spirit at Pentecost. This is, however, no mere historical remembrance. Through the celebration of the liturgy the same Holy Spirit manifests the exalted Lord continually in his church, keeping alive the promise of Jesus that he would be with us until the end of time. Easter and Pentecost are the centre of the life of grace by which God adopts us as his children. They are our victory over death.

Prayer

> Lord our God, by the resurrection of your Son,
> you have forever illumined the world.
> Through the power of your Spirit,
> grant that those who still sit in darkness
> and in the shadow of death,
> may be born anew,
> and that your light may shine on them
> for ever and ever. Amen.

Green or Ordinary Time

The time after Easter (and between Christmas time and Lent) is called 'ordinary time', but for the Christian, no time is merely ordinary. The Spirit of Pentecost, poured out on the church, has filled the whole world with the glory of the risen Christ. The church lives his mysteries in her Sunday celebration of the Eucharist, in which Easter and Pentecost are manifested anew. The vestments are green to signify the new life welling up in the world through the action of God's Holy Spirit.

Prayers

For feasts of Christ

God of heaven and earth,
Through Jesus you have made known to us
the name of Father,
The Word who was made flesh,
And the person of the Holy Spirit.
May you be blessed for opening to us
The secret of your inmost life,
And for inviting us to enter it
In the glory where you reign
For ever and ever.

Prayer for feasts of Mary

Lord our God,
You have wrought marvels
in Mary, your lowly handmaid.
May our weakness and our poverty
ever manifest the power of your grace,
through Jesus, your Son, our Lord.

Prayer for saint(s) of the day

We give you thanks, our Lord and God,
for saint(s) N,
and the unnumbered company of witnesses
whose prayer and love surround us.
May they, although unseen,
sustain and strengthen us
on our journey towards your light,
Jesus Christ, our Lord.

SECTION TWO

Familiar Prayers

The Sign of the Cross

In the name of the Father, and of the Son, and of the Holy Spirit. Amen.

In ainm an Athar agus an Mhic agus an Spioraid Naoimh. Amen.

In nomine Patris, et Filii, et Spiritus Sancti. Amen.

Prayer of Praise

Glory be to the Father, and to the Son, and to the Holy Spirit, as it was in the beginning, is now, and ever shall be, world without end. Amen.

Glóir don Athair, agus don Mhac, agus don Spiorad Naomh, mar a bhí ar dtús, mar atá anois, agus mar a bheas go brách le saol na saol. Amen.

Gloria Patri et Filio et Spiritui Sancto, sicut erat in principio et nunc et semper, et in saecula saeculorum. Amen.

The Lord's Prayer

   Our Father, who art in heaven,
   hallowed be thy name.
   Thy kingdom come.
   Thy will be done
   on earth as it is in heaven.
   Give us this day our daily bread,
   and forgive us our trespasses
   as we forgive those
   who trespass against us,
   and lead us not into temptation,
   but deliver us from evil. Amen.

   Ár n-Athair atá ar neamh,
   Go naofar d'ainm.
   Go dtaga do ríocht.
   Go ndéantar do thoil ar an talamh
   mar a dhéantar ar neamh.
   Ár n-arán laethúil tabhair dúinn inniu,
   agus maith dúinn ár bhfiacha
   mar a mhaithimidne dár bhféichiúna féin,
   agus ná lig sinn i gcathú,
   ach saor sinn ó olc. Amen.

   Pater noster, qui es in caelis,
   sanctificetur nomen tuum.
   Adveniat regnum tuum.
   Fiat voluntas tua, sicut in caelo, et in terra.
   Panem nostrum quotidianum da nobis hodie,
   et dimitte nobis debita nostra
   sicut et nos dimittimus debitoribus nostris,

et ne nos inducas in tentationem,
sed libera nos a malo.

The Hail Mary

Hail Mary, full of grace,
the Lord is with thee.
Blessed art thou among women,
and blessed is the fruit of thy womb, Jesus.
Holy Mary, Mother of God,
pray for us sinners now
and at the hour of our death. Amen.

'Sé do bheatha, a Mhuire,
atá lán de ghrásta,
tá an Tiarna leat.
Is beannaithe thú idir mná,
agus is beannaithe toradh do bhroinne, Íosa.
A Naomh-Mhuire, a Mháthair Dé,
guigh orainn na peacaigh
anois agus ar uair ár mbáis. Amen.

Ave Maria, gratia plena
Dominus tecum.
Benedicta tu in mulieribus,
et benedictus fructus ventris tui Jesus.
Sancta Maria, Mater Dei,
ora pro nobis peccatoribus nunc
et in hora mortis nostrae.
Amen.

Memorare

> Remember, O most loving Virgin Mary,
> that it is a thing unheard of
> that anyone ever had recourse to your protection,
> implored you help, or sought your intercession,
> and was left forsaken.
> Filled therefore with confidence in your goodness,
> I fly to you, O Mother, Virgin of virgins,
> to come to you, before you I stand, a sorrowful sinner.
> Despise not my poor words, O Mother of the Word of
> God,
> but graciously hear and grant my prayer. Amen

The Apostles' Creed

> I believe in God, the Father almighty,
> creator of heaven and earth.
>
> I believe in Jesus Christ, his only Son, our Lord,
> who was conceived by the power of the Holy Spirit
> and born of the Virgin Mary.
> He suffered under Pontius Pilate,
> was crucified, died, and was buried.
> He descended to the dead.
> On the third day he rose again.
> He ascended into heaven,
> and is seated at the right hand of the Father.
> He will come again to judge the living and the dead.
>
> I believe in the Holy Spirit,
> the holy Catholic Church,
> the communion of saints,

the forgiveness of sins,
the resurrection of the body,
and the life everlasting. Amen.

Act of Contrition

O my God I am sorry for all my sins
Because they offend you who are so good
And with your help I will not sin again.

Guardian Angel Prayer

Angel of God, my Guardian dear
to whom God's love commits me here.
Ever this day be at my side
to light and guard to rule and guide.
Amen.

The Jesus Prayer – Prayer of the Heart

Lord Jesus Christ, Son of God,
have mercy on me a sinner.

Prayer to the Holy Spirit

Come Holy Spirit, fill the hearts of your faithful
and kindle in them the fire of your love.
Send forth your Spirit and they shall be created,
And you shall renew the face of the earth.

St Patrick's Breastplate

I bind unto myself today
the power of God to hold and lead,
his eye to watch, his might to stay,
his ear to harken to my need:
the wisdom of my God to teach,
his hand to guide, his shield to ward;
the word of God to give me speech,
his heavenly host to be my guard.

Christ be with me, Christ before me,
Christ behind me, Christ deep within me,
Christ below me, Christ above me,
Christ at my right hand, Christ at my left hand,
Christ as I lie down, Christ as I arise,
Christ as I stand,
Christ in the heart of everyone who thinks of me,
Christ in the mouth of everyone who speaks to me,
Christ in every eye that sees me,
Christ in every ear that hears me.

Gléasaim mé féin inniu
i neart Dé do mo luamhaireacht;
i gcumhact Dé do mo choinneáil;
i gciall Dé do m'iomthús;
i rosc Dé do mo réamhfheiceáil;
i gcluas Dé do m'éisteacht;
i mbriathar Dé do m'urlabhairt;
i láimh Dé do m'imdheaghail;
in inteach Dé do mo réamhtheacht;

i sciath Dé do m'imdhídean;
i sochraidí Dé do m'anacal.

Críost liom, Críost romham,
Críost i mo dhiaidh, Críost istigh ionam,
Críost fúm, Críost os mo chionn,
Críost ar mo láimh dheas, Críost ar mo láimh chlé,
Críost i mo luí dhom, Críost i mo shuí dhom,
Críost i mo sheasamh dhom,
Críost i gcroí gach duine atá ag cuimhneamh orm,
Críost i mbéal gach duine a labhraíonn liom,
Críost i ngach súil a fhéachann orm,
Críost i ngach cluais a éisteann liom.

Prayer of St Francis
   Lord, make me an instrument of your peace:
      where there is hatred let me sow love,
      where there is injury let me sow pardon,
      where there is doubt let me sow faith,
      where there is despair let me sow hope,
      where there is darkness let me give light,
      where there is sadness let me give joy.
   O divine master, grant that I may
      not try to be comforted but to comfort,
      not try to be understood but to understand,
      not try to be loved but to love.
   For it is in giving that we receive,
      it is forgiving that we are forgiven,
      and it is dying that we are born to eternal life.

The Rosary

Christians have recited the Rosary for centuries. The Rosary developed in parallel with the Monastic Office with its 150 psalms mirroring the 150 Hail Marys of the Rosary cycle. This cycle outlines the history of salvation from the announcement of Christ's birth to Mary's coronation in heaven.

Many religions use beads to quiet the mind. The repetition of prayers and the handling of beads creates a space allowing the Spirit to whisper through our spirit, 'Glory be to the Father'.

The Rosary begins by blessing oneself with the cross and saying the Apostles' Creed. On the first bead, the Our Father is said and on the next three beads three Hail Marys, followed by Glory be to the Father. There follow three groups of five 'mysteries', each with its own salvific event for meditation. Each mystery, or decade, begins with the Our Father, followed by ten Hail Marys, concluding with the Glory be to the Father. It ends with the Hail Holy Queen and a prayer.

The Joyful Mysteries

Traditionally said on Monday and Thursday and Sundays of Advent.

1. The Annunciation

Then Mary said, 'Here am I, the servant of the Lord; let it be with me according to your word.' (Lk 1:38)

2. The Visitation

And blessed is she who believed that there would be a fulfilment of what was spoken to her by the Lord. (Lk 1:45)

3. The Birth of Our Lord

The angel said to them, 'Do not be afraid, for see – I am bringing you good news of great joy for all the people: to you is born this day in the city of David a saviour, who is the Messiah, the Lord.' (Lk 2:10-12)

4. The Presentation in the Temple

Now, Master, you can let your servant go in peace just as you promised, because my eyes have seen the salvation which you have prepared for all the nations to see. (Lk 2:29)

5. The Finding of Jesus in the Temple

Why were you looking for me? Did you not know that I must be in my Father's house? But they did not understand what he meant. (Lk 2:49-50)

The Sorrowful Mysteries

Traditionally said on Tuesday and Friday and Sundays of Lent

1. The Agony in the Garden.

Father , if you are willing, remove this cup away from me; yet, not my will but yours be done. (Lk 22:42, 43)

2. The Scourging at the Pillar

So Pilate, wishing to satisfy the crowd, released Barabbas for them; and after flogging Jesus, he handed him over to be crucified. (Mk 15:15)

3. The Crowning with Thorns

And the soldiers wove a crown of thorns and put it on his head, and they dressed him in a purple robe. (Jn: 19:2)

4. The Carrying of the Cross.

After mocking him, they stripped him of the robe and put his own clothes on him. Then they led him away to crucify him. (Mt 27:31)

5. The Crucifixion

When they came to the place that is called The Skull, they crucified Jesus there with the criminals, one on his right and one on his left ... Then Jesus, crying out with a loud voice, said, 'Father, into your hands I commend my spirit.' Having said this, he breathed his last. (Lk 23:33, 46)

The Glorious Mysteries

Traditionally said on Wednesday, Saturday and Sundays of Advent

1. The Resurrection

The angel said to the women, 'Do not be afraid; I know that you are looking for Jesus who was crucified. He is not here; for he has been raised, as he said.' (Mt 28:5-6)

2. The Ascension

When he had said this, as they were watching, he was lifted up, and a cloud took him out of their sight. (Acts 1: 9)

3. The Coming of the Holy Spirit.

And suddenly from heaven there came a sound like a rush of a violent wind, and filled the entire house where they were sitting. Divided tongues as of fire appeared among them, and a tongue rested on each of them. All of them were filled with the Holy Spirit. (Acts 2:2-4)

4. The Assumption of Mary into Heaven.

Listen, I will tell you a mystery! We will not all die, but we will all be changed, in a moment, in the twinkling of an eye, at the last trumpet. For the trumpet will sound, and the dead will be raised imperishable, and we will be changed. (1 Cor 15:51-52)

5. The Coronation of Our Lady Queen in Heaven

A great portent appeared in heaven: a woman clothed with the sun, with the moon under her feet, and on her head a crown of twelve stars. (Rev 12:1)

Hail, Holy Queen, Mother of Mercy!
Hail, our life, our sweetness, and our hope!
To thee do we cry, poor banished children of Eve;
to thee do we send up our sighs,
mourning and weeping in this valley of tears.
Turn, then, most gracious advocate,
thine eyes of mercy toward us,
and after this our exile
show unto us the blessed fruit of thy womb, Jesus;
O clement, O loving, O sweet Virgin Mary.

V. Pray for us, O Holy Mother of God.
R. That we may be made worthy of the promises of Christ.

Let us pray:
O God,
whose only begotten Son,
by his life, death, and resurrection,
has purchased for us the rewards of eternal life,
grant, we beseech thee,
that meditating upon these mysteries
of the Most Holy Rosary of the Blessed Virgin Mary,
we may imitate what they contain and obtain what they
promise, through the same Christ Our Lord. Amen.

The Angelus

In the name of the Father, and of the Son, and of the Holy Spirit. Amen.

V. The angel of the Lord declared unto Mary.

R. And she conceived of the Holy Spirit.

Hail Mary

V. Behold the handmaid of the Lord.

R. Be it done unto me according to your word.

Hail Mary

V. And the Word was made flesh.

R. And dwelt among us.

Hail Mary

V. Pray for us, O Holy Mother of God.

R. That we may be made worthy of the promises of Christ.

From Easter Sunday until Pentecost, the following is said in place of the above verses and responses:

O Queen of heaven, rejoice, alleluia,

For he whom you were worthy to bear, alleluia,

Has risen as he said, alleluia.

Pray for us to God, alleluia.

Let us pray:

Pour forth, we beseech you, O Lord,

your grace into our hearts;

that, we to whom the incarnation of Christ, your Son,

was made known by the message of an angel,

may by his passion and cross,

be brought to the glory of his resurrection.

Through Christ our Lord. Amen.

The Stations of the Cross

For centuries, pilgrims travelled to the Holy Land visiting the sites associated with Jesus' death and resurrection. Once home, they represented these sites in their churches, as 'stations' or the Way of the Cross. The stations helped them to meditate on the passion of Jesus. They can do the same for us today.

1. Jesus is condemned to death

Pilate said to them, 'Take him and crucify him; I find no case against him.' (Jn 19:6)

> Lord Jesus Christ, you accepted an unjust judgement. Give us the grace to remain faithful to the truth. To you, O Jesus, just Judge, be honour and glory for ever and ever. Amen

2. Jesus takes up his cross

For God so loved the world that he gave his only Son, so that everyone who believes in him may not perish but may have eternal life. (Jn 3:16)

> Lord Jesus Christ, you accepted the cross to make it a sign of God's love for humanity: grant us faith in this infinite love. To you, O Jesus, Priest and Victim, be praise and glory for ever. Amen.

3. Jesus falls the first time

All we like sheep have gone astray; we have all turned to our own way, and the Lord has laid on him the iniquity of us all. (Is 53:6)

O Christ, as you fall under the weight of the cross, we pray, help us and all who are weighed down by sin to stand up again and continue the journey. To you, O Jesus, crushed under the weight of our faults, be our praise and love for ever. Amen.

4. Jesus meets his mother

Here am I, the servant of the Lord; let it be with me according to your word. (Lk 1:38)

O Mary, you walked the way of the cross with your son. You were fully confident that he to whom nothing is impossible would fulfil his promises: implore for us the grace to surrender to God's love.

To Jesus, your son, honour and glory for ever and ever. Amen.

5. Simon helps Jesus carry his cross.

They compelled a passer-by, who was coming in from the country, to carry his cross; it was Simon of Cyrene.' (Mk 15:21)

O Christ, you gave to Simon of Cyrene the dignity of carrying your cross. Grant to everyone the gift of readiness to serve.

To you, O Jesus, who bore the cross, be praise and glory for ever. Amen.

6. Veronica wipes the face of Jesus

By pouring this ointment on my body she has prepared me for burial. (Mt 26:12)

> Lord Jesus Christ, you accepted a woman's selfless gesture of love. Grant that our works will show to the world a reflection of your infinite love.
>
> To you, O Jesus, splendour of the Father's glory, be praise and glory for ever. Amen.

7. Jesus falls the second time

But I am a worm, and not human; scorned by others, and despised by the people. (Ps 22:6)

> Lord Jesus Christ, you fall under the weight of human sin and rise again to cancel it. Give to us the strength to carry the cross, that we may proclaim the gospel of your saving power.
>
> To you, O Jesus, our support when we are weak, be praise and glory for ever. Amen.

8. Jesus consoles the women of Jerusalem

But Jesus turned to them and said, 'Daughters of Jerusalem, do not weep for me, but weep for yourselves and for your children.' (Lk 23:28)

> O Christ, you came into this world to visit those who await salvation: grant that we will recognise the time of your visitation and share in your redeeming grace.
>
> To you, O Jesus, born of the Virgin Daughter of Zion, be honour and praise for ever and ever. Amen

9. Jesus falls the third time

And being found in human form, he humbled himself and became obedient to the point of death – even death on a cross. (Phil 2:7-8)

Lord Jesus Christ, through your humiliation on the cross you revealed to the world the price of its redemption. Grant us the light of faith, that we may follow the same path which leads to life without end.

To you, O Jesus, our support when we are weak, be honour and glory for ever and ever. Amen.

10. Jesus is stripped and offered gall and vinegar to drink

They offered him wine to drink, mixed with gall; but when he tasted it he would not drink it. (Mt 27:34)

Lord Jesus, you accepted death on the cross for our salvation: grant us to glory in your sacrifice that we may share in your work of salvation.

To you, O Jesus, Priest and Victim, be honour and glory for ever. Amen.

11. Jesus is nailed to the cross

And I, when I am lifted up from the earth, will draw all people to myself. (Jn 12:32)

O Christ raised up on the cross, fill our hearts with your love, that we may see in it the sign of our redemption, who live and reign with the Father and the Spirit, now and for ever.

To you, O Jesus, who died on the cross, be praise and glory for ever. Amen.

12. Jesus dies on the cross

Jesus, remember me when you come into your kingdom.
Father into your hands I commend my spirit.
(Lk 23:42 & 46)

> Lord Jesus, you entrusted to the Father's mercy the people
> of every age. Fill us with your Spirit of love, so that our
> indifference will not render vain the fruits of your death.
> To you, crucified Jesus, the wisdom and the power of
> God, be honour and glory for ever. Amen.

13. Jesus is taken down from the cross and is given to his
mother

His mother treasured all these things in her heart. (Lk 2:51)

> Mary, our mother, implore for us the grace of faith,
> hope and love, so that we, like you, may stand without
> flinching beneath the cross.
> To your Son, Jesus our Saviour, with the Father and the
> Holy Spirit, all honour and glory for ever and ever. Amen.

14. Jesus is laid in the tomb

Unless a grain of wheat falls into the earth and dies, it
remains just a single grain; but if it dies, it bears much fruit.
(Jn 12:24)

> Lord Jesus Christ, in the Holy Spirit you were drawn
> from the darkness of death to the light of new life.
> Grant that your empty tomb may be for us a source of
> faith, hope and love.
> To you, O Jesus, whose presence, hidden and victorious,
> fills the history of the world, be honour and glory for
> ever and ever. Amen.

SECTION THREE   RITUAL PRAYERS

Prayers For Various Occasions

1. A short act of devotion to our Holy Father Benedict,
   Patriarch of Monks

   The following prayers can be said by Benedictine
   Oblates, or simply by those who wish to invoke the
   assistance and protection of the saint.

V. Lord open my lips,

R. and my mouth shall proclaim your praise!

   Glory to you, Christ our King, glory to you!

   Support me, O Lord, according to your word and I shall
   live!

   Let me not be disappointed in my hope.

   Glory be to the Father, and to the Son and to the Holy
   Spirit.

   Support me, O Lord, according to your word and I shall
   live!

V. St Benedict, our patron, pray for us:

R. that we may be made worthy of the promises of Christ.

Let us pray: *(silence)*

   Rekindle in your church, Lord, the Spirit whom our
   holy father Benedict followed and obeyed: filled with
   the same Spirit may we love what he loved and live as he
   taught us, through Christ our Lord. Amen

V. St Scholastica, pray for us:

R. that in all things God may be glorified.

Let us pray: *(silence)*

Eternal God, by whose grace Scholastica became a burning and shining light for your people: give us courage to prefer nothing to Christ. By the power of the Holy Spirit, help us to share patiently in his sufferings, that we may be able to rejoice forever in his kingdom. We ask this through Christ our Lord. Amen.

Prayer for a happy death

Lord our God, who filled the blessed Abbot Benedict with the Spirit of Christ and made him an outstanding teacher of the gospel, (on his feastdays, add 'on this festival of his return to you' [21 March] or 'as we implore his intercession for all who are dedicated to God [11 July]), lead us on the way of your love. At the end of our earthly life, grant us through his prayers a happy death and receive us into your heavenly kingdom to rejoice with him in glory.

2. In the morning

Éirím suas le Dia	I arise with God,
go n-éirí Dia liom.	may God rise with me.
Lámh Dé i mo thimpeall,	God's hand enfolding me
ag suí is ag luí	as I sit, as I lie down
's ag éirí dom.	and as I arise.

Traditional, Mayo

3. In the evening

An Triúr is sine, and Triúr is óige,
an Triúr is treise i bhflaitheas na glóire,
an tAthair, an Mac is an Spiorad Naomh
do m' shábháil, do m' ghardáil
ó anocht go dtí bliain ó anocht
agus anocht féin.

To the Most Holy Trinity, ever ancient, ever new,
ever powerful in heavenly splendour:
Father, Son and Holy Spirit,
be my saving and my guarding
from tonight until a year from tonight,
and especially tonight.

4. Before engaging in any work

A Íosa ionúin, toirbhrim mé féin duit idir anam agus
chorp
Mar aon leis an obair seo.
A Íosa, a mhilse mo chroí, tabhair grá lasúin dom ort.
A Íosa, mo dhóigh is mo shólás, tabhair dom do thoil a
dhéanamh.
A Muire, a Mháthair na ngrás,
neartaigh agus cuidigh liom.

O beloved Jesus, along with this work of this day
I dedicate myself to you in soul and body.
O Jesus, treasure of my heart, make ardent my love for you.
O Jesus, my hope and my comforting joy, let me do your
will always.
Mary, mother of grace, strengthen and help me.

5. Prayer for peace and tranquillity

My Lord Jesus Christ,
may your peace be with me.
In you, O Jesus, true peace,
may I have peace upon peace eternally.
Through you may I come to that peace
which surpasses all understanding,
there where, in gladness, I may see you in yourself.
Amen.

St Gertrude of Helfta

Let nothing ever disturb you,
Nothing affright you;
All things are passing,
God never changes.
Patient endurance
Attains to all things;
Who God possesses
In nothing is wanting:
Alone God suffices.

St Teresa of Avila

6. Prayers for guidance

May God, the Lord, bless us and make us perfect and
holy in his sight. May the riches of his glory abound in
us. May he instruct us with the word of truth, inform us
with the gospel of salvation, and enrich us with his love;
through Christ our Lord.

Gelasian Sacramentary

Bless all who worship you, almighty God, from the rising of the sun to its setting: from your goodness enrich us, by your love inspire us, by your Spirit guide us, by your power protect us, in your mercy receive us, now and always.

Ancient Collect

Dear Lord, give me the truths which are veiled by the doctrines and articles of faith, which are masked by the pious words of sermons and books. Let my eyes penetrate the veil, and tear off the mask, that I can see your truth face to face.

St John of the Cross

Steer the ship of my life, good Lord, to your quiet harbour, where I can be safe from the storms of sin and conflict. Show me the course I should take. Renew in me the gift of discernment, so that I can always see the right direction in which I should go. And give me the strength and the courage to choose the right course, even when the sea is rough and the waves are high, knowing that through enduring hardship and danger we shall find comfort and peace.

Saint Basil of Caesarea

7. Beannacht ar chách ('Blessing on everyone')

Nara tiugha féar ag fás
Ná gaineamh ar thrá
Ná drúcht ar bhán
Ná na beannachtaí ó Rí na ngrás
Ar gach anam a bhí, a bheidh ná atá.

Not more generous the growing blades of grass
Nor the grains of sand on the shore
Nor the dewdrops on the pasture
be the blessings of the King of grace
on every soul that was, that will be or that is.

8. Blessings before and after meals

Grace before meals

1. Bless, O Lord, the food and drink of your servants, for you are merciful, now and forever. Amen.

2. Bless us, O Lord, and these your gifts which of your goodness we are about to receive through Jesus Christ our Lord. Amen.

3. Blessed are you, Father, who give us our daily bread. Blessed is your only begotten Son who continually feeds us with the word of life.
Blessed is the Holy Spirit, who brings us together at this table of love.
Blessed be God now and for ever.
Amen.

4. Beannaigh sinne, a Dhia,
Beannaigh ár mbia agus ár ndeoch.
Ós tú a cheannaigh sinn go daor agus a shaor sinn ó olc;
agus mar thug tú an chuid seo dúinn
go dtuga tú dúinn ár gcuid den ghlóir shíoraí.

Traditional, Tyrone

Bless us, O God, bless our food and drink.
You who so dearly bought us and saved us from sin.
And since you give us our share now,
may you give us our share in your glory hereafter.

Grace after meals

1. We give you thanks, almighty God, for these and for all your blessings, who live and reign for ever and ever. Amen.

2. We thank you, Christ our Lord, for sharing your blessing with us: fill us also with the gifts of your grace. Amen.

3. We give you thanks, holy Lord, our Father,
for your loving gifts of food and drink.
Grant that one day we may sit at the table of your heavenly kingdom and there sing a hymn of praise to you for ever. Amen

4. Moladh le Rí na reann, moladh go hard leat, a Dhia,
moladh le hÍosa Críost a thug dúinn an bia.
De réir mar do thug sé an bia dúinn ar an talamh seo,
go dtuga sé an bheatha shíoraí dúinn sna flaithis.

Traditional, Clare

Praise to you, the King of the highest, the greatest praise
to you, O God,
praise to Jesus Christ who gave us food.
Just as he gives food on this earth,
may he give us everlasting life in heaven.

9. Prayer in time of sickness or with one who is sick

Rí an Domhnaigh mo dhochtúir-se
Is Muire liaigh dom leighis
's a chroch neamh gan róchuirsi
go sgairid mé / thú rem / red theinnis.

Richard Butler, 15th century Anglo Norman poet

May the King of Sunday, my doctor
and Mary my physician in my illness,
and the holy cross, grant that without too great sorrow
  I / you shall be parted from my illness.

10. Prayer before travelling

Leanfad thú, a Thiarna, pé áit dá ngeobhair, de bhrí gur
agatsa atá briathra na beatha síoraí.

Traditional, Louth

I shall follow you, O Lord, any place you go, because it
is you who have the words of eternal life.

11. When visiting a cemetery

Go mbeannaí Dia daoibh, a fhoireann,
go mbeannaí Dia daoibh agus Muire.
Bhí sibhse tamall mar atá sinne,
Beimidne fós mar atá sibhse.
Go rabhaimid go léir fé mhaise
Ag Rí geal na cruinne.

Traditional, Waterford

May God bless all the company of souls here,
may God and Mary bless you.
You too spent awhile here just as we are now
and we too will join you soon.
May we all be adorned in the beauty
of the bright King of heaven.

12. Communion prayers

Son of the Living God,
Lord Jesus Christ,
whose death
willed by the Father, empowered by the Holy Spirit,
restored the life of the world,
deliver me from all my iniquities and from every evil
through this most sacred Body and Blood of yours,
keep me always close to your commandments
and never allow me be separated from you.

Latin original from 9th century

Lord Jesus Christ,
let not the receiving of your Body and Blood
turn to my judgement and condemnation.
Rather, in your love let it be for me
a defence of mind and body,
a remedy to be taken.

Latin original 10th century

Lord, in your wonderful sacrament you have left us a memorial of your death and resurrection. Teach us so to reverence these sacred mysteries of your Body and Blood that we may perceive within ourselves and show forth in our lives the fruits of our redemption, for you are alive and reign, Father, Son and Holy Spirit, for ever and ever. Amen

St Thomas Aquinas

Father, we thank you who have planted
your holy name within our hearts.
Knowledge and faith and life immortal
Jesus your Son to us imparts.

You Lord, have made all for your pleasure,
You give us food for all our days,
Giving in Christ the bread eternal;
Yours is the power, and yours the praise.

Watch over your church, O Lord, in mercy,
Save it from evil, guard it still,
Perfect it in your love, unite it,
Cleansed and conformed unto your will.

As grain, once scattered on the hillsides,
Was in this broken bread made one,
So from all lands, may your church be gathered
into your kingdom by your Son.

From prayers in the 'Didache', 2nd century

Sancti, venite

Draw near and take the body of the Lord,
and drink with faith the blood for you outpoured.

Offered was he for greatest and for least,
Himself the Victim, and himself the Priest.

He that his saints in this world rules and shields
To all believers life eternal yields.

He feeds the hungry with the bread of heaven
And living streams to those who thirst are given

Approach you then with faithful hearts sincere,
and take the pledges of salvation here.

Ireland, 7th century

Prayer to our Redeemer

Soul of Christ, make me holy,
Body of Christ, be my salvation.
Blood of Christ, let me drink your wine.
Water flowing from the side of Christ, wash me clean.
Passion of Christ, strengthen me.
Kind Jesus, hear my prayer;
hide me within your wounds
and keep me close to you.
Defend me from the evil enemy.
Call me at my death
to the fellowship of your saints,
so that I may sing your praise with them
through all eternity. Amen.

The Roman Missal

13. Prayers of self-dedication

Dearest Lord, teach me to be generous:
Teach me to serve you as you deserve;
To give and not to count the cost,
To fight and not to heed the wounds,
To toil and not to seek for rest,
To labour and not to ask for any reward
Save that of knowing that I do your will.

St Ignatius of Loyola

Receive, Lord, all my liberty, my memory, my understanding and my whole will. You have given me all that I have, all that I am, and I surrender all to your divine will, that you dispose of me. Give me only your love and your grace. With this I am rich enough and I have no more to ask.

St Ignatius of Loyola

14. Prayer in difficult times

At least – to pray – is left – is left –
Oh Jesus – in the Air –
I know not which thy chamber is –
I'm knocking – everywhere –

Thou settest Earthquake in the South –
And Maelstrom, in the Sea –
Say, Jesus Christ of Nazareth –
Hast thou no arm for me?

Emily Dickinson

Blessings

For the following Blessings, a leader (L) is chosen from the group. The rest of the group (P) respond.

1. Blessing of a home

L: In the name of the Father and of the Son and of the Holy Spirit.

P: Amen

L: Peace be with this house and all who live here.

Reading

Whatever house you enter, first say, 'Peace to this house!' And if anyone is there who shares in peace, your peace will rest on that person; but if not it will return to you … cure the sick who are there, and say to them, 'The kingdom of God has come near to you.' (Lk 10:5-6, 9)

L: Lord we ask you to bless those who live in this home.
Be their shelter when they are at home,
their companion when they are away,
and their welcome guest when they return.
And at last receive them into the dwelling place
you have prepared for them in your Father's house,
where you live for ever and ever.

P: Amen

L: *Sprinkles house with holy water and says the following:*
Let this water bless this house and call to mind our baptism into Christ who has redeemed us by his death and resurrection.

P: Amen

L: May the peace of Christ reign in our hearts and may the word of Christ in all its richness dwell in us, so that whatever we do in word or work we will do in the name of the Lord.

P: Amen

2. Blessing of a family

L: In the name of the Father and of the Son and of the Holy Spirit.

P: Amen

L: Peace be with this house and all who live here.

P: And also with you.

Reading

As God's chosen ones, holy and beloved, clothe yourselves with compassion, kindness, humility, meekness and patience. Bear with one another and if anyone has a complaint against another, forgive each other, just as the Lord has forgiven you, so you also must forgive. Above all, clothe yourselves with love, which binds everything together in perfect harmony. And let the peace of Christ rule in your hearts, to which indeed you were called in the one body. (Col 3:12-15)

L: Lord, we ask you to bestow on this family the riches of your blessing. With the gift of your grace, sanctify those who live here, so that, faithful to your commandments, they will care for each other, ennoble this world by their lives, and reach the home you have prepared for them in heaven. We ask this through Christ our Lord.

P: Amen

L: May the God of hope fill you with every joy in believing. May the peace of Christ abound in your hearts. May the Holy Spirit enrich you with his gifts, now and forever.

P: Amen

3. Blessing of the elderly

L: In the name of the Father and of the Son and of the Holy Spirit.

P: Amen

L: The grace and peace of God our Father and the Lord Jesus Christ be with you all.

P: And also with you.

Reading

Rejoice in the Lord always; again I will say, Rejoice. Let your gentleness be known to everyone. The Lord is near. Do not worry about anything, but in everything, by prayer and supplication with thanksgiving, let your requests be made known to God. And the peace of God, which surpasses all understanding, will guard your hearts and your minds in Christ Jesus. (Phil 4:4-5)

L: Lord, our God, you have given N. the grace to maintain hope in you through all life's changes and to taste and see your goodness. We bless you for the gifts you have showered on him/her. We ask that he/she may find joy in renewed strength of spirit, that he/she may have good health, and that he/she may inspire us by the example of his/her life. We ask this through Christ our Lord.

P: Amen

L: And may almighty God bless you all, the Father, and the Son and the Holy Spirit.

P: Amen

4. Blessing on the occasion of a death

L: In the name of the Father and of the Son and of the Holy Spirit.

P: Amen

L: May the Father of mercies, the God of all consolation, be with you all.

P: And also with you.

Reading

Come to me all you that are weary and are carrying heavy burdens, and I will give you rest. Take my yoke upon you, and learn from me, for I am gentle and humble in heart, and you will find rest for your souls. For my yoke is easy, and my burden is light. (Mt 11:28-30)

L: Lord our God, the death of N. recalls our human condition and the brevity of our lives on earth. But for those who believe in your love, death is not the end, nor does it destroy the bonds that you forge in our lives. We share the faith of your Son's disciples and the hope of the children of God. Bring the light of Christ's resurrection to this time of testing and pain as we pray for N. and for those who love him/her, through Christ our Lord.

P: Amen

L: May the peace of God which is beyond all understanding keep your hearts and minds in the knowledge and love of God and of his Son, our Lord Jesus Christ.

P: Amen

L: And may almighty God bless you, the Father, and the Son and the Holy Spirit.

P: Amen

5. Blessing of a sick person

L: In the name of the Father and of the Son and of the Holy Spirit.

P: Amen

L: Peace be with you.

P: And also with you.

L: As we prepare to pray, we keep in mind the words of scripture which tell us how God anointed Jesus with the Holy Spirit and with power, and how he went about healing everyone.

Reading

When Jesus entered Peter's house, he saw his mother-in-law lying in bed with a fever; he touched her hand, and the fever left her, and she got up and began to serve him. That evening they brought to him many who were possessed by demons; and he cast out the spirits with a word, and cured all who were sick. This was to fulfil what had been spoken through the prophet Isaiah, 'He took our infirmities and bore our diseases.' (Mt 8:14-17)

L: Lord and Father, almighty and eternal God, by your blessing you give us strength and support in our frailty: turn with kindness toward your servant N. Free him/her from all illness and restore him/her to health, so that in the sure knowledge of your goodness he/she will gratefully bless your holy name. We ask this through Christ our Lord.

P: Amen

L: May God the Father bless you.

P: Amen

L: May God the Son comfort you.

P: Amen

L: May God the Holy Spirit enlighten you.

P: Amen

L: And may almighty God bless you, the Father, and the Son and the Holy Spirit.

P: Amen

6. Blessing going on a journey

L: In the name of the Father and of the Son and of the Holy Spirit.

P: Amen

L: Our help is in the name of the Lord.

P: Who made heaven and earth

Reading

 I lift up my eyes to the hills;
from where will my help come?
My help comes from the Lord
who made heaven and earth.

The Lord will keep you from all evil;
he will keep your life.
The Lord will keep your going out and your coming in
from this time on and forevermore.

Glory be.

L: Gracious God, in whom we live and move and have our
being, be with us, throughout the course of this journey, so
that, under your protecting hand, we may reach our destination in safety, through Jesus, the Christ, our Lord.
P: Amen
L: And may almighty God bless you, the Father, and the
Son and the Holy Spirit.
P: Amen

7. Blessing of a person in need of inner healing
L: In the name of the Father and of the Son and of the
Holy Spirit.
P: Amen
L: May the grace and peace of Christ be with you.
P: And also with you.

Reading
But now thus says the Lord, he who created you, O Jacob
he who formed you, O Israel: Do not fear, for I have
redeemed you; I have called you by name, you are mine.
When you pass through the waters, I will be with you; and
through the rivers, they shall not overwhelm you; when
you walk through fire you shall not be burned, and the
flame shall not consume you. For I am the Lord your God,
the Holy One of Israel, your Saviour. (Is 43:1-3)

L: Ever faithful God, you sent into the darkness of our lives your Son Jesus Christ, the light of the world. Stretch forth your healing hand over N. your servant. Give him/her serenity of mind and peace of heart. Raise him/her up in body, soul and spirit and deliver him/her from all evil. We make our prayer through Jesus, the Christ, our Lord.

P: Amen

L: May God the Father bless you.

P: Amen

L: May God the Son comfort you.

P: Amen

L: May God the Holy Spirit enlighten you.

P: Amen

L: And may almighty God bless you, the Father, and the Son and the Holy Spirit.

P: Amen

8. Blessing for the dead when visiting a cemetery

L: In the name of the Father and of the Son and of the Holy Spirit.

P: Amen

L: May the grace and peace of Christ be with you.

P: And also with you.

Reading

Out of the depths, I cry to you, O Lord,

Lord, hear my voice!

Let your ears be attentive

to the voice of my supplications.

If you, O Lord, should mark our iniquities,
Lord, who could stand?
But there is forgiveness with you,
so that you may be revered.

And with him is great power to redeem.
It is he who will redeem Israel
from all its iniquities. (Psalm 130)

L. Eternal rest grant unto them O Lord,
P. And let perpetual light shine upon them.

L: O God, our creator and redeemer, grant to all the souls
of your departed servant(s) buried in this sacred space the
pardon which they have always desired. You comforted
Mary and Martha on the death of their brother Lazarus.
Console those who mourn the passing of these, our brothers and sisters.

O Holy Spirit, who by your power raised Jesus to life again,
bring us to that day of our resurrection when we will be
united once again with those whom we love in the unend-
ing happiness of the kingdom of God.

We make these prayers, O God, through Jesus Christ our
Lord who lives and reigns united to you by the Holy Spirit,
for ever and ever.

P: Amen

L. Eternal rest grant unto them, O Lord,
P. And let perpetual light shine upon them.
L. May their souls, and the souls of all the faithful departed,
through the mercy of God, rest in peace.
P. Amen.

SECTION FOUR ADDITIONAL PSALMS

Psalm 35

Sin whispers to sinners
in the depths of their hearts.
There is no fear of God before their eyes.

They so flatter themselves in their minds
that they know not their guilt.
In their mouths are mischief and deceit,
all wisdom is gone.

They plot the defeat of goodness as they lie in bed.
They have set their feet on evil ways,
they cling to what is evil.

Your love, Lord, reaches to heaven;
your truth to the skies.
Your justice is like God's mountain,
your judgments like the deep.

To mortals and beasts you give protection.
O Lord, how precious is your love.
My God, the children of the earth
find refuge in the shelter of your wings.

They feast on the riches of your house;
they drink from the stream of your delight.
In you is the source of life
and in your light we see light.

Keep on loving those who know you,
doing justice for upright hearts.
Let the foot of the proud not crush me
nor the hand of the wicked cast me out.

See how the evil-doers fall!
Flung down they shall never arise.

Psalm 117

Give thanks to the Lord
for he is good
for his love endures forever.

Let the family of Israel say:
'His love endures forever.'
Let the family of Aaron say:
'His love endures forever.'
Let those who fear the Lord say:
'His love endures forever.'

I called to the Lord in my distress;
he answered and freed me.
The Lord is at my side; I do not fear.
What can mortals do against me?
The Lord is at my side as my helper:
I shall look down on my foes.

It is better to take refuge in the Lord
than to trust in mortals:
It is better to take refuge in the Lord
than to trust in rulers.

The nations all encompassed me;
in the Lord's name I crushed them.
They compassed me, compassed me about;
in the Lord's name I crushed them.

They compassed me about like bees;
they blazed like a fire among thorns.
In the Lord's name I crushed them.

I was thrust down, thrust down and falling
but the Lord was my helper.
The Lord is my strength and my song;
he was my saviour.
There are shouts of joy and victory
in the tents of the just.

The Lord's right hand has triumphed;
his right hand raised me.
The Lord's right hand has triumphed
I shall not die, I shall live
and recount his deeds.
I was punished, I was punished by the Lord,
but not doomed to die.

Open to me the gates of holiness:
I will enter and give thanks.
This is the Lord's own gate
where the just may enter.
I will thank you for you have answered
and you are my saviour.

The stone which the builders rejected
has become the corner stone.
This is the work of the Lord,
a marvel in our eyes.
This day was made by the Lord;
we rejoice and are glad.

O Lord, grant us salvation;
O Lord, grant success.
Blessed in the name of the Lord is he who comes.
We bless you from the house of the Lord;
the Lord God is our light.

Go forward in procession with branches
even to the altar.
You are my God, I thank you.
My God, I praise you.
Give thanks to the Lord for he is good;
for his love endures for ever.

Psalm 145

My soul, give praise to the Lord:
I will praise the Lord all my days,
make music to my God while I live.

Put no trust in the powerful,
mere mortals in whom there is no help.
Take their breath, they return to clay
and their plans that day come to nothing.

They are happy who are helped by Jacob's God,
whose hope is in the Lord their God,
who alone made heaven and earth,
the seas and all they contain.

It is the Lord who keeps faith forever,
who is just to those who are oppressed.
It is God who gives bread to the hungry,
the Lord, who sets prisoners free,

the Lord who gives sight to the blind,
who raises up those who are bowed down,
the Lord, who protects the stranger
and upholds the widow and orphan.

It is the Lord who loves the just
but thwarts the path of the wicked.
The Lord will reign forever,
Zion's God from age to age.

Psalm 146

Praise the Lord for he is good;
sing to our God for he is loving;
to him our praise is due.

The Lord builds up Jerusalem
and brings back Israel's exiles,
he heals the broken hearted,
he binds up all their wounds.
He fixes the number of the stars;
he calls each one by its name.

Our Lord is great and almighty;
his wisdom can never be measured.
The Lord raises the lowly;
he humbles the wicked to the dust.
O sing to the Lord, giving thanks;
sing psalms to our God with the harp.

He covers the heavens with clouds;
he prepares the rain for the earth,
making mountains sprout with grass
and with plants to serve our needs.
He provides the beasts with their food
and young ravens that call upon him.

His delight is not in horses
nor his pleasure in warriors' strength.
The Lord delights in those who revere him,
in those who wait for his love.

Psalm 147

O praise the Lord, Jerusalem!
Zion, praise your God!

He has strengthened the bars of your gates,
he has blessed the children within you.
He established peace on your borders,
he feeds you with finest wheat.

He sends out his word to the earth
and swiftly runs his command.
He showers down snow white as wool,
he scatters hoarfrost like ashes.

He hurls down hailstones like crumbs,
the waters are frozen at his touch;
he sends forth his word and it melts them;
at the breath of his mouth the waters flow.

He makes his word known to Jacob,
to Israel his laws and decrees.
He has not dealt thus with other nations;
he has not taught them his decrees.

Psalm 148

Praise the Lord from the heavens,
praise him in the heights.
Praise him all his angels,
praise him all his hosts.

Praise him sun and moon,
praise him shining stars.
Praise him highest heavens
and the waters above the heavens.

Let them praise the name of the Lord.
He commanded, they were made.
He fixed them for ever,
gave a law which shall not pass away.

Praise the Lord from the earth,
sea creatures and all oceans,
fire and hail, snow and mist,
stormy winds that obey his word;

All mountains and hills,
all fruit trees and cedars,

Beasts, wild and tame,
reptiles and birds on the wing;

All earth's nations and peoples,
earth's princes and rulers;
Young men and maidens,
the old together with children.

Let them praise the name of the Lord
for he alone is exalted.
The splendour of his name
reaches beyond heaven and earth.

He exalts the strength of his people.
He is the praise of all his saints,
of the sons and daughters of Israel,
of the people to whom he comes close.

Psalm 150

Praise God in his holy place,
praise him in his mighty heavens.
Praise him for his powerful deeds,
praise his surpassing greatness.

O praise him with sound of trumpet,
praise him with lute and harp.
Praise him with timbrel and dance,
praise him with strings and pipes.

O praise him with resounding cymbals,
praise him with clashing of cymbals.
Let everything that lives and that breathes,
give praise to the Lord. Alleluia!

SECTION FOUR

READINGS FROM THE RULE OF ST BENEDICT

Hear and heed my son the master's teaching and bow the ear of your heart. Willingly take to yourself the father's advice and fulfil it in what you do. Thus by laborious obedience will you return to him, from whom you have withdrawn by idle disobedience.

RB Prologue

Let us open our eyes to the divine light, and with startled ears let us listen to what the divine voice is calling out every day, urging us: Today if you should hear his voice, harden not your hearts.

RB Prologue

As for him who is making progress in the religious life and in faith, his heart opens wide and with the joy that is too great for words and which comes from love, he runs ahead in the way of God's commandments.

RB Prologue

Let monks therefore exercise this zeal with burning love, that is, let them anticipate one another with honour. And with utmost patience bearing their weaknesses whether of bodies or of characters let them vie with one another in rendering mutual obedience.

RB 6

What could be sweeter, beloved brothers than this voice of the Lord, who is inviting us? See, in his loving kindness, the Lord points out to us the path of life.

RB Prologue

Do everything with consultation and you will have no regrets when the deed is done.

RB 3

To speak and to teach, indeed, befits the master; to be silent and to listen becomes the disciple.

RB 6

To be on the fourth rung of humility is to embrace patience, silently and consciously.

RB 7

A man is recognised as wise when his words are few.

RB 7

...the Morning and Evening Office should never come to a close without the Lord's Prayer being said in full at the end ... on account of the thorny scandals which have a habit of springing up so that, challenged by the promise of the very prayer itself in which they say: 'Forgive us as we forgive', they may purge themselves of this kind of vice.

From holy Easter until Pentecost alleluia shall be said without exception.

RB 13

Let us so stand at psalmody that mind and voice may be in tune.

RB 19

If when making suggestions to men in power we do not venture to do so except with humility and deference, how much more ought supplication be made to the Lord, God of all, with all humility and pure devotion. And let us realise that we shall be heard not in much speaking, but in purity of heart, in compunction and tears. And that is why a prayer should be brief and pure, unless perhaps it be pro-longed by an inspiration of divine grace.

RB 20

Nothing indeed is so unsuited to any Christian as over-eat-ing, as our Lord says: 'Take heed to yourselves lest your hearts be overburdened with self-indulgence.'

RB 39

... if ... he wishes to pray more secretly by himself, let him in all simplicity go in and pray, not with a loud voice but with tears and an attentive heart.

RB 52

All guests who appear shall be welcomed as Christ ... let Christ be worshipped in them: he is being welcomed.

It is most especially in the reception of the poor and of pilgrims that attentive care is to be shown, because in them Christ is all the more received. Dread is enough of itself to secure honour for the rich.

RB 53

Let no one seek his own interests but those of his neighbour. Let them with purity offer the love of brotherhood. Let them fear God lovingly.

RB 72

Let them prefer absolutely nothing to Christ. May he bring us all alike to everlasting life.

RB 72

… what page or phrase of divine authority of the Old and New Testament is not the straightest norm for a human life? Or what book of the holy Catholic Fathers does not re-echo how we may reach our Creator in a straight run?

RB 73

Calendar of Saints and Feasts

From among the thousands of recorded saintly personalities, we have chosen a selection of appropriate guardian saints for each day. These represent various ages, cultures and continents.

Saints are the real historical proof both of God's love for us on the one hand, and the genuine possibility of transformation which that same love, through Jesus Christ, promises on the other. Through a daily remembrance and celebration of our foreparents in prayer, our very beings can be gently sculpted and moulded into true witnesses of the salvific scheme of Christ. Furthermore, in recalling these people of prayer as models of the message of the gospels, we too are profoundly challenged by them. Pertinent to their time in history, these holy ones interpreted and lived out the Christian message in a new, radical and courageous manner. The universal vocation to sainthood calls us towards that same pure fusion of the mundane and the spiritual at this crucial time. Keenly observing these delicate dancers of holiness, we can, in turn, follow their sacred steps and take our earthly place in that spiritual union which the Christian creed names as *'communio sanctorum'*, 'the communion of saints'.

In entrusting our daily round of prayers, petitions and protection to such powerful mediators, who themselves have done God's will throughout the ages, we reiterate the ultimate Christian quest enshrined in the prayer of the eucharist: 'to share eternal life with Mary, the Virgin Mother of God, with the apostles and all the saints …'

January / Eanáir

1 Solemnity of Mary, mother of God / St Odilo, France, d. 1048

2 Sts Basil and Gregory, Asia Minor, d. 379 / d.c. 389

3 St Munchin, Mainchín, Ireland, 7th century / St Genevieve, France, d. 500 – patron of Paris

4 St Elizabeth Ann Seton, USA, d. 1821

5 St John Neumann, USA, d. 1860

6 The Epiphany of the Lord / Blessed Andre Bessette, Canada, d. 1936

7 St Raymond of Pennafort, Spain, d. 1275

8 St Severinus, apostle of Austria, d. 482

9 St Adrian of Canterbury, Africa, d. 710

10 St Peter Orseolo, Italy d. 987 / St Diarmuid, Dermot, Ireland, 6th century

11 St Theodosius, Asia Minor, d. 529

12 St Benedict Biscop, England, d. 690

13 St Hilary of Poitiers, France, d.c. 368

14 St Felix of Nola, Italy, d. 260

15 St Ita, Íde, Ireland, d. 570 / Sts Maur and Placid, Italy, d. 6th century

16 St Fursa, Ireland, d. 648

17 St Anthony, Egypt, d. 356 – patriarch of monks

18 Prisca, friend to St Paul, 1st century

19 St Wulfstan, England, d. 1095

20 St Fabian, Italy, d.c. 250 / St Sebastian, Italy, d. 304

21 St Agnes, Italy, d.c. 304

22 St Vincent, Spain, d. 304

23 St John the Almsgiver, Egypt, d.c. 619

24 St Francis de Sales, France, d. 1622

25 The Conversion of St Paul of Tarsus, Asia Minor, d.c. 67

26 Sts Robert, Alberic and Stephen, England, 12th century /
   Sts Timothy and Titus, Asia Minor, d. 97

27 St Angela Merici, Italy, d. 1540

28 St Thomas Aquinas, Italy, d. 1274

29 St Gildas the Wise, England, d. 570

30 St Aidan, Aodán, Ireland, d. 626

31 St John Bosco, Italy, d. 1888 – patron of youth

February / Feabhra

1   St Brigid, Bríd, Ireland, d. 524 – secondary patron of
    Ireland, patron of poetry, healing and smithscraft

2   The Presentation of the Lord / Candlemas / St Joan of
    Lestonnach, France, d. 1640

3   St Blaise, Armenia, West Asia, d.c. 315 – protector of
    throats / St Ansgar, France, d. 865

4   St John de Britto, Spain, d. 1693

5   St Agatha, Italy, d.c. 251

6   St Paul Miki and companions, Japan, d. 1597 (USA Feb 5)

7   St Mel, England, 5th century

8   St Jerome Emiliani, Italy, d. 1537

9   St Ansbert, France, d.c. 695

10 St Scholastica, twin sister of St Benedict, Italy, d.c. 542

11 Our Lady of Lourdes / St Gobnait, Ireland, 7th century /
    St Benedict of Aniane, Gaul, W. Europe, 9th century

12 St Alexander of Alexandria, Egypt, d. 328

13 St Catherine dei Ricci, Italy, d. 1590

14 Sts Cyril and Methodius, Greece, d. 869, 885 / St
    Valentine, Italy, d.c. 269 – patron of lovers

15 Blessed Jordan of Saxony, Italy, d. 1237

16 St Onesimus, Italy, 1st century

17 St Fintan, Fiontán, Ireland, d. 549/Seven Holy Founders of the Servite Order, Italy, 13th century

18 St Flavian, Constantinople, d. 449/St Colmán of Lindisfarne, Ireland, d. 676

19 St Boniface of Lausanne, France, d. 1265

20 St Wulfric, England, d. 1154

21 St Peter Damian, Italy, d. 1072

22 The Chair of St Peter. (The chair *(cathedra)* symbolises the episcopal office, in this case that of the Bishop of Rome, the Pope.)

23 St Polycarp, Asia Minor, d.c. 155

24 St Walburga, England, d. 779

25 St Ethelbert of Kent, England, d. 616

26 St Alexander, Egypt, d. 328

27 St Gabriel of Our Lady of Sorrows, Italy, d. 1862

28 St Oswald, England, d. 992

29 St Justus, England, d. 627

March/Márta

1   St David, England, d. 589 – patron of Wales

2   St Chad, England, d. 672

3   St Marinus of Caesarea, Israel, d.c. 262 / St Katharine Drexel, USA, d. 1955

4   St Casimir, Poland, d. 1484

5   St Ciarán of Saighir, Ireland, 5th/6th century

6   St Colette, Belgium, d. 1447

7   Sts Perpetua and Felicity, Africa, d. 203

8   St Senan, Ireland, d. 544/St John of God, Spain, d. 1550 – patron of nurses and the sick

9 St Frances of Rome, Italy, d. 1440 – patron of widows

10 St John Ogilvie, England, d. 1615

11 St Aengus, Ireland, d.c. 824

12 St Maximilian, Africa, d. 295

13 St Euphrasia, Egypt, d.c. 412

14 St Leobinus, France, d. 558

15 St Louise de Marillac, France, d. 1660 – patron of social workers

16 St Finnian, Ireland, d.c. 560

17 St Patrick, Ireland, d. 461 – patron of Ireland

18 St Cyril of Jerusalem, Palestine, d. 386

19 St Joseph, 1st century – patron of the church and husbands

20 St Cuthbert, England, d. 687

21 The Passing of St Benedict, Italy, d.c. 550/St Enda, Ireland, d.c. 520

22 St Nicholas Owen, England, d. 1606

23 St Turibius, Spain, d. 1606 – patron of native rights

24 St Macartan, Ireland, d.c. 505/St Catherine of Sweden, d. 1381

25 The Annunciation of the Lord / William of Norwich, England, d. 1144

26 St Braulio, Spain, d. 651

27 St John of Egypt, d. 394

28 St Tutilo OSB, Switzerland, d. 915

29 St Rupert, Germany, d.c. 710

30 St John Climacus, Palestine, d.c. 649

31 St Benjamin, Persia, 5th century

April / Aibreán

1   St Hugh of Grenoble, France, d. 1132 / St Ceallach, Ireland, d. 1129

2   St Francis of Paola, Italy, d. 1507

3   Sts Agape, Chionia and Irene, Greece, d. 304

4   St Isidore, Spain, d. 636

5   St Vincent Ferrer, Spain, d. 1419 – patron of builders

6   St Celestine, Italy, d. 432

7   St John-Baptist de la Salle, France, d. 1719 – patron of teachers

8   St Dionysius of Corinth, Greece, 2nd century

9   St Mary of Egypt, 5th century

10 St Terence, Africa, 3rd century

11 St Gemma Galgani, Italy, d. 1903 / St Stanislaus, Poland, d. 1097

12 St Zeno of Verona, Italy, d. 371 – invoked to help children walk and talk

13 St Martin I, Italy, d. 655

14 St Justin, Palestine, d.c. 165 – patron of philosophers

15 St Ruadar of Lorrha, Ireland, d.c. 584

16 St Bernadette of Lourdes, France, d. 1879

17 St Stephen Harding, England, d. 1134

18 St Apollonia of Alexandria, Egypt, d. 249 / St Laserian, Ireland, d. 639

19 St Alphege of Canterbury, England, d. 1012

20 St Beuno, England, 7th century

21 St Anselm, England, d. 1109

22 St Soter, Italy, 2nd century

23 St George, England, d.c. 300 – patron of England / St Adelbert of Prague, Czechoslovakia, d. 997

24 St Fidelis of Sigmaringen, Germany, d. 1622

25 St Mark the evangelist, 1st century

26 St Cletus, Italy, 2nd century

27 St Asicus, Irish, 5th century / St Zita, Italy, d. 1278

28 St Peter Chanel, France, d. 1841 / St Louis Mary de
   Montfort, France, d. 1716

29 St Catherine of Siena, Italy, d. 1380 – co-patron of
   Europe

30 St Pius V, Italy, d. 1572

May / Bealtaine

1 St Joseph the Worker, 1st century – patron of workers

2 St Athanasius, Alexandria, d. 373

3 Sts Philip and James, apostles, 1st century

4 St Conleth, Ireland, 5th century

5 Blessed Edmund Ignatius Rice, Ireland, d. 1844

6 St Edbert, England, d. 698

7 St John Beverly, England, d. 721

8 Julian of Norwich, England, d. 1423

9 St Gerontius, Italy, d. 501

10 St Comgall, Ireland, d.c. 605

11 St Francis di Girolamo, Italy, d. 1766

12 St Pancras, Italy, 4th century – patron of children /
   Ss Nereus and Achilleus, Italy, d.c. 100

13 Blessed Imelda, Italy, d. 1333

14 St Matthias, apostle, 1st century

15 St Carthage, Ireland, d. 638 / St Pachomius, Egypt,
   d.c. 346 / St Isidore, Spain, d. 1130

16 St Brendan the navigator, Ireland, d. 578

17 St Paschal Baylon, Spain, d. 1592

18 St John I, Italy, d. 526

19 St Celestine, Italy, d. 1296 / St Dunstan, England, d. 988

20 St Bernardine of Siena, Italy, d. 1444

21 St Andrew Bobola, Poland, d. 1623

22 St Rita, Italy, d. 1457

23 St William of Rochester, England, d. 1154

24 St David of Scotland, England, d. 1153 / Our Lady Help of Christians – patroness of Australia

25 St Bede the venerable, England, d. 735 – patron of scholars / St Gregory VII, Italy, d. 1085 / St Mary Magdalene of Pazzi, Italy, d. 1607

26 St Philip Neri, Italy, d. 1595

27 St Augustine of Canterbury, England, d. 604

28 St Germanus of Paris, France, d. 576

29 St Maximinus, Constantinople, d. 662

30 St Joan of Arc, France, d. 1431 – patron of France and of radio

31 The Visitation of the Virgin Mary

June / Meitheamh

1 St Justin, Palestine, d.c. 165 – patron of philosophers

2 Sts Marcellinus and Peter, Italy, d. 303

3 St Kevin of Glendalough, Ireland, d.c. 618

4 Sts Charles Lwanga and companions, Uganda, d. 1886 (USA Jun 3)

5 St Boniface, England, d.c. 754

6 St Jarlath, Ireland, 6th century / St Norbert, Netherlands, d. 1134

7 St Colman of Dromore, Ireland, 6th century

8 St William of York, England, d. 1154

9 St Colm Cille, Ireland, d. 597 – patron of Glenstal Abbey / St Ephrem, Syria, d. 373

10 St Celulius, Italy, 3rd century

11 St Barnabas, Cyprus, 1st century

12 St John of Sahagun, Spain, d. 1479

13 St Anthony of Padua, Italy, d. 1231

14 St Methodius of Constantinople, d. 847

15 St Vitus, Italy, d.c. 305 – patron of dancers

16 St Aurelian, France, d.c. 548

17 St Besarion, Egypt, 4th century

18 St Elizabeth of Schönau, Germany, d. 1164

19 St Juliana Falconieri, Italy, d. 1341/St Romuald, Italy,
      d. 1027

20 St Alban, England, d.c. 209

21 St Aloysius Gonzaga, Italy, d. 1568 – patron of youth

22 St Paulinus of Nola, France, d. 431 / St John Fisher and
      St Thomas More, England, d. 1535

23 St Agrippina, Italy, 3rd century

24 Birth of St John the Baptist, 1st century

25 St William of Vercelli, Italy, d. 1142

26 St Anthelm, France, d. 1178

27 St Cyril of Egypt, d. 444

28 St Irenaeus, Asia Minor, d.c. 202

29 Sts Peter and Paul, apostles, 1st century

30 Protomartyrs of the Roman Church, 1st century

July / Iúil

1   St Oliver Plunkett, Ireland, d. 1681 / Blessed Junipero
      Serra, Spain, d. 1784

2   St Otto of Bamberg, d. 1139

3   St Thomas, apostle, 1st century

4   St Elizabeth of Portugal, Spain, d. 1336

5 St Anthony Zaccaria, Italy, d. 1539

6 St Moninne of Killeavy, Ireland, d.c. 517/St Maria Goretti, Italy, d. 1902

7 St Maolruain, Ireland, d. 792

8 St Procopius, Palestine, d. 303/St Killian, Ireland, d.c. 689

9 St John of Rochester, England, d. 1535

10 Sts Alexander and the six martyr sons of St Felicity, Italy, 3rd century

11 St Benedict, Italy, d. 550 – patron of Europe

12 St John Gualberto, OSB Italy, d. 1073

13 St Henry, Germany, d. 1024

14 St Camillus de Lellis, Italy, d. 1614 – patron of hospitals and the sick / St Kateri Tekakwitha, North America, d. 1680

15 St Bonaventure, Italy, d. 1274

16 Our Lady of Mount Carmel

17 St Alexis, Syria, 5th century

18 St Frederick, Italy, d. 1190 / St Camillus de Lellis, Italy, d. 1614

19 St Arsenius Italy, d.c. 412

20 St Jerome Emiliani, Italy, d. 1537

21 St Lawrence of Brindisi, Germany, d. 1619

22 St Mary Magdalene, 1st century

23 St Bridget of Sweden, d. 1373 – patron of Europe/St John Cassian, Eastern Europe, d. 435

24 St Declan, Déaglán, Ireland, 6th century

25 St James, apostle, 1st century

26 Sts Joachim and Anne, parents of Mary, 1st century

27 St Theobald, England, d. 1161

28 St Nazarius, Italy, d.c. 395

29 St Martha, 1st century – patron of housewives

30 St Peter Chrysologus, Italy, d.c. 450

31 St Ignatius of Loyola, Spain, d. 1556

August/Lúnasa

1 St Alphonsus Liguori, Italy, d. 1787

2 St Peter Julian Eymard, France, d. 1868 / St Eusebius of Vercelli, Sardinia, d. 371

3 St Germanus of Auxerre, France, d. 448

4 St John Vianney, France,d. 1859 – patron of priests

5 St Anthony Zaccaria, Italy, d. 1539 / Dedication of Mary Major

6 The Transfiguration of the Lord

7 St Sixtus II and companions, Italy, d. 258

8 St Dominic, Spain, d. 1221 / Blessed Mary McKillop, Australia, d. 1909

9 St Teresa Benedicta of the Cross, Edith Stein, Germany, d. Auschwitz, 1942 – co-patron of Europe

10 St Lawrence, Italy, d. 258 – patron of the poor

11 St Clare, Italy, d. 1253

12 St Attracta, Ireland, 6th century

13 St Fachtna Ireland, d.c. 600 / St Pontian and St Hippolytus, Italy, 3rd century

14 St Maximilian Kolbe, Poland, d. Auschwitz, 1941

15 The Assumption of Mary

16 St Stephen of Hungary, d. 1038

17 St Hyacinth, Silesia, c. Europe, d. 1257

18 St Helen, Asia Minor, d.c. 330

19 St John Eudes, Normandy, Italy, d. 1680/ St Bernard Tolomei, Italy, d. 1348

20 St Bernard, France, d. 1153 – patron of bee-keepers and candlemakers

21 St Pius X, Italy, d. 1914

22 The Queenship of Mary

23 St Eugene, Eoghan, Ireland 6th century / St Rose of Lima, Peru, d. 1617

24 St Bartholomew, apostle, 1st century

25 St Louis IX, King of France, d. 1270 / St Joseph Calasanz, Spain, d. 1648

26 St Elizabeth Bichier des Ages, France, d. 1838

27 St Monica, Africa, d. 387 – patron of mothers

28 St Augustine of Hippo, Africa, d. 430 – patron of theologians

29 The Beheading of St John the Baptist, 1st century

30 St Fiacre, Ireland / France, d.c. 670 – patron of gardeners

31 St Aidan of Lindisfarne, England, d. 651

September / Meán Fómhair

1 St Giles, France, 8th century – patron of physically disabled

2 St Stephen, King of Hungary, d. 1038

3 St Gregory the Great, Italy, d. 604 – patron of singers

4 St Oengus Mac Neasa, Ireland, 6th century

5 St Lawrence Giustiniani, Italy, d. 1455

6 St Bega, Ireland / England, 7th century

7 St Adrian, Italy, d.c. 306 / St Cloud, England, 7th century

8 The Nativity of the Virgin Mary / St Adrian, d. 304

9 St Ciaran of Clonmacnoise, Ireland, d. 545 / St Peter Claver, Spain, d. 1654

10 St Nicholas of Tolentino, Italy, d. 1305

11 St Deiniol, England, 6th century

12 St Ailbe, Ireland, d. 528

13 St John Chrysostom, Greece, d. 407 – patron of preachers

14 Triumph of the Cross

15 Our Lady of Sorrows / St Catherine of Genoa, d. 1510

16 St Cornelius, Italy, d. 253 / St Cyprian, Africa, d. 258

17 St Hildegard OSB, Germany, d. 1179 / St Robert
Bellarmine, Italy, d. 1621

18 St Joseph of Cupertino, Italy, d. 1663 – patron of air
travellers

19 St Januarius, Italy, d.c. 305

20 St Andrew Kim and Companions, Korea, 19th century

21 St Matthew the apostle, 1st century

22 St Maurice, Egypt, 3rd century

23 St Adamnan or Eunan, Ireland, d. 704

24 Our Lady of Ransom / St Gerard Csanad, Italy, d. 1046

25 St Finbar, Ireland, d.c. 633

26 Sts Cosmos and Damian, Syria, d.u. – patrons of
physicians

27 St Vincent de Paul, France, d. 1660 – patron of all
charitable works

28 St Wenceslaus, Germany, d. 925 / St Lawrence Ruiz and
companions, Philippines, 17th century

29 Sts Michael, Gabriel and Raphael Archangels

30 St Jerome, Dalmatia, Yugoslavia, d. 420 – patron of
librarians and students

October/Deireadh Fómhair

1   St Thérèse of Lisieux, France, d. 1897 – patron of
France, the church's missions and florists

2   The Guardian Angels

3   Blessed Columba Marmion, Ireland, d. 1923

4   St Francis of Assisi, Italy, d. 1226 – patron of ecologists

5   Blessed Raymond of Capua, Italy, d. 1399

6   St Bruno, Germany, d. 1101 / Blessed Marie Rose
    Durocher, Canada, d. 1849

7   Our Lady of the Rosary

8   St Pelagia of Antioch, Turkey, d.c. 304 / St Bridget of
    Sweden, d. 1373

9   St Denis / Dionysius of Paris, France, d.c. 258 / St John
    Leonardi, Italy, d. 1609

10 St Francis Borgia, Spain, d. 1572

11 St Canice, Ireland, d.c. 603

12 St Wilfrid, England, d. 709

13 St Edward the Confessor, England, d. 1066

14 St Callistus, Italy, d.c. 222

15 St Teresa of Avila, Spain, d. 1582

16 St Gall, Ireland, d.c. 630 / St Hedwig OSB, Germany,
    d. 1243 / St Margaret Mary Allacoque, France, d. 1690

17 St Ignatius of Antioch, Turkey, d.c. 107

18 St Luke evangelist, Greece, 1st century – patron of
    artists and of doctors

19 St Paul of the Cross, Italy, d. 1775 / Ss Isaac Jogues,
    France, d. 1647 and John de Brébeuf, France, d. 1648,
    and companions, 17th century

20 St Irene of Portugal, Spain, d. 304 / St Andrew of Crete,
    d.c. 371

21 St Fintan of Taghmon, Ireland, d. 635

22 St Donatus, Ireland, d. 876

23 St John of Capistrano, Italy, d. 1456

24 St Anthony Claret, Spain, d. 1870

25 Forty Martyrs of England and Wales, 16/17th centuries

26 St Cedd, England, d. 664

27 St Otteran, Ireland, d. 548

28 Sts Simon and Jude apostles, 1st century

29 St Colman of Kilmacduagh, Ireland, d.c. 632

30 St Marcellus, the centurion, martyr, Italy, d. 298

31 St Wolfgang, Germany, d. 994

November/Samhain

1 All Saints

2 All Souls

3 St Malachy, Ireland, d. 1148/St Martin de Porres, Peru,
   d. 1639 – patron of justice

4 St Charles Borromeo, Italy, d. 1584

5 Sts Elizabeth and Zacharia, 1st century, parents of John
   the Baptist

6 All Saints of Ireland

7 St Willibrord, England, d. 739

8 All Saints of Wales

9 Dedication of Saint John Lateran Basilica, Rome

10 St Leo the Great, Italy, d. 461

11 St Martin of Tours, Hungary, d. 397

12 St Josaphat, Russia, d. 1623

13 St Francis Xavier Cabrini, Italy, d. 1917

14 St Laurence O'Toole, Ireland, d. 1180

15 St Albert the Great, Italy, d. 1280 – patron of scientists

16 St Gertrude OSB, Germany, d. 1302/St Margaret of
Scotland d.1093

17 St Elizabeth of Hungary d. 1231

18 St Mawes, England, 6th century / Dedication of
    Cathedral of Sts Peter and Paul, Rome

19 St Mechtilde of Magdeburg, Germany, d.c. 1282

20 St Edmund, England, d. 869

21 The Presentation of the Virgin Mary

22 St Cecilia, Italy, d.u. – patron of music and musicians

23 St Columban, Ireland, d. 615 / St Clement I, Italy, d.c.
    100 / Blessed Miguel Augustine Pro, Mexico, d. 1927

24 St Colman of Cloyne, Ireland, d. 604 / St Andrew
    Dung-Lac and Companions, Vietnam, d. 1839

25 St Katherine of Alexandria,Egypt, 4th century – patron
    of students

26 St Leonard, Italy, d. 1751

27 St Fergus, Ireland, d. 784

28 St Catherine Labouré, France, d. 1876

29 St Saturninus, Syria, 2nd century

30 St Andrew apostle, 1st century – patron of Scotland

December / Nollaig

1   St Eligius, France, d. 660 – patron of veterinarians

2   St Viviana, Italy, d.u.

3   St Francis Xavier, Spain, d. 1552 – patron of missionaries

4   St John Damascene, Syria, d. 749

5   St Sabas, Turkey, d. 532

6   St Nicholas of Myra, Turkey, 4th century – patron of
    Russia and children

7   St Ambrose, Italy, d. 397 – patron of domestic animals

8   The Immaculate Conception of the Virgin Mary

9   St Peter Fourier, France, d. 1640 / Blessed Juan Diego,
    Mexico, d. 1548

10 St Gregory III, Pope, Rome, d. 741

11 St Damasus, Italy, d. 384

12 St Jane Frances de Chantal, France, d. 1641/St Finnian of
   Clonard, Ireland, d. 549 / Our Lady of Guadalupe,
   Mexico

13 St Lucy, Italy, d. 304

14 St John of the Cross, Spain, d. 1591

15 St Valerian, Italy, d.u./St Paul of Latros, Bithynia, d. 956

16 St Adelaide, Burgundy, France, d. 999

17 St Olympias, Constantinople, d.c. 408

18 St Flannan, Ireland, 7th century

19 St Anastasius, Egypt, d.c. 700

20 St Dominic of Silos, Spain, d. 1073

21 St Peter Canisius, Netherlands, d. 1597

22 Blessed Jutta, Germany, d. 1136

23 St John Kanty, Poland, d. 1473

24 St Tharsilla, Italy, d.c. 550

25 The Nativity of the Lord

26 St Stephen, Palestine, d.c. 35 – patron of deacons

27 St John the Evangelist, 1st century

28 The Holy Innocents, 1st century / St Eugenia, Rome

29 St Thomas à Becket, England, d. 1170

30 St Egwin, England, d.c. 717

31 St Sylvester, Italy, d. 335